The Colored Folks Ain't Gonna Make It

Volume 2 from the **Sketches of Lee** *Collection*

By Michael Cameron Ward

Dedication

This volume of Sketches of Lee, "The Colored Folks Ain't Gonna Make It," is dedicated to my late brother, Beverly Theodore Ward. His guidance, friendship, and love were not always apparent, but I have come to realize that they were, and remain, an integral part of my consciousness. They are also part of the legacy of the future "Ward Boys." Be tough, be fair, and keep your own counsel.

Thanks Teddy. I'll see you on the other side.

Semper Fi,

Mike

FASTEN YOUR SEATBELT!

Introduction

I'm an accidental author. Before my father, Harold Ward, passed on June 9, 2015, he and I had several long talks about the major events of our family's life and times. We have a strong oral history, even as memories have been lost over the generations. He wanted his seven grandchildren and nine great grandchildren to know "from whence they came." He asked me to make sure that the sacrifices he and my mother Virginia made were not forgotten.

1945 - Harold and Virginia - 2006

Most of these stories have never been told outside of our family. Some of them have an edge, some are funny, some are not, but all of them are real. In some cases, the lessons learned were not revealed until much later in life. The crux of many of these accounts was how our race affected, or didn't affect, the progression of relatively "normal" family events. It is worth noting that 15 of the 40 plus stories have nothing to do with race.

Many of our friends and neighbors were under the impression that we had somehow transcended the issue of race. We had not. However, allowing that to become common knowledge would have revealed weakness. We could not at any cost risk exposing this to individuals who wished us ill. In writing and circulating these memoirs, some of my oldest friends have expressed shock and anger that I had not shared our difficulties as they occurred. To that, I have only one response: The demands of our friendship cannot supersede the survival of my family.

While I was performing preview performances of this book, I made a discovery. Our experiences as the index of integration weren't unique. There is an intersection of experience with all of those of a particular race or religion who were the first ones on the block.

The only real names used are mine, Harold's, Virginia's, my brother Ted's, deceased individuals, or people who did something totally exceptional. Descriptions of the actions of morons, buffoons, and jerks are rendered in the third person. My sister's names were omitted because they did not wish to be included in the project.

In some cases, unnamed folks who had a positive impact are identifiable by distinguishing characteristics. If so, I contacted them or their family and read them the story. If they didn't approve, it was archived or modified such that the point was not lost. My intention is to illustrate our experience, not to beat someone like a drum.

Sadly, the person who should have been my fellow raconteur, my brother Ted, passed away on July 9, 2014. So, it's up to me to reflect and relate some of the more critical junctures of our journey. And no, I do not need jumper cables to restart my memory.

Mom and Dad were not perfect. They relied on trial, error, advice, and determination. There is nothing that breeds respect in New Hampshire like determination. They had the latter and earned the former.

Michael Cameron Ward

The Colored Folks Ain't Gonna Make It

The arrival of the Ward family in Lee, New Hampshire from Brooklyn, New York was akin to a Mars landing. There was nothing with which we were familiar. Every thought or activity was the inverse of our Brooklyn experience: similar on its face, underneath, wholly different. Or, as my father Harold once noted, in what became the town joke of the Sixties: "Until we got here, Lee, New Hampshire was whiter than the North Pole."

In 1957, my father, Harold E. Ward, was deployed with the U.S. Navy's Atlantic Fleet on AE17, "the Great Sitkin." At the same time back in Brooklyn, our neighborhood underwent a change for the worse. The newly emergent gang activity made our living environment untenable. Dad couldn't protect us. My 13-year-old brother Ted and I, age 3, had both been beaten up by gang members. Then one afternoon, a man was discovered peering in a bedroom window at one of my sisters. To Mom and Dad that was confirmation that my two sisters, in between Ted and me in age, had become targets.

We had to move, but where?
Do you go south to: "The devil you know?"
Do you go north to: "The devil you don't know?"

Moving south was not an option. Segregation was still the law of the land. Dad's experiences with segregation in the

U.S. Navy and Emmitt Till's lynching in Mississippi two years before had rendered it a moot point.

In 1955, Dad's second cousin, Vivian Richardson, and her husband, Benjamin, had relocated from New Jersey to New Hampshire. Ben had auditioned for and was selected to be the organist at St. John's Church at the foot of the Memorial Bridge in Portsmouth. They suggested that we consider the New Hampshire seacoast area. There was little overt racism, and in general the atmosphere was a welcoming one.

In 1956, "Cousin Viv" became the first Colored teacher in the newly formed Oyster River School District in Durham, New Hampshire.

Dad was a Commissaryman Petty Officer First with 18 years of shipboard and wartime service. He checked out housing at the Portsmouth Naval Shipyard. Although the armed forces were integrated, we could not live on the base. Dad was not a submariner; there was a shortage of housing for submariners; and, we were "Colored."

In the meantime, Cousin Ben and Vivian's bed and breakfast for Colored city folks, Solar Vista, had failed. It was too far. A 14-hour drive up Route 1 from Metropolitan New York through hostile territory was just too much for their friends and associates. As a point of reference, think of the 2019 Oscar winner for Best Picture, "The Green Book."

They offered the house and property to us. With no other
viable options, Mom and Dad rolled the dice. They sold our
house at 362 Grand Avenue in Brooklyn, purchasing Ben and
Vivian's with the proceeds. On July 14, 1957, our family of
six relocated to Solar Vista on Big Hook Road, a two-lane
strip of dirt in Lee, New Hampshire.

Solar Vista and the '49 Mercury

Vivian was always sharp financially. She socked it to us,
charging 20% more than the market rate. When my mother
found out, she was not happy. Then again, we ended up with
quite a package: a nine-room house and garage, a four-story
chicken barn, a sandpit, a 75 by 250 yard hayfield, ⅛ mile of
frontage on the Lamprey River, and two wells, sprawled
across 82 acres of land, for the outrageous sum of $17,500.

Dad hung a picture of the house above his bunk on the Great Sitkin. A chief petty officer from down south saw it. He froze and asked Dad, "Is that your house?"

"Yes, it's up in New Hampshire. We just moved in."

The chief's face turned red. He turned, left, and never spoke to Dad again.

New Hampshire is one tough place to live, especially when you have to learn how to heat your house and raise your own food. To describe Solar Vista as "cold" in the winter and our first harvests as "meager" greatly undervalues the meaning of both terms.

The winters of 1957 through '59 were particularly brutal. Originally, Solar Vista was a barn. In 1957, it was still barnlike. There was no insulation, but it did have an oil furnace and a giant coal stove in the basement. Oil was too expensive, so we kept the thermostat at 50 degrees. If you were caught turning it up, you were spanked, and hard. We couldn't afford coal, so we primarily heated the house with wood.

One cold winter afternoon, I remember helping Mom and Ted drag some large branches through the snow into the basement. The three of us were smiling because we would be warm that night. Ted cut them up with a handsaw and put them into the stove.

A big surprise was in store for the city people: wood must be dry to burn. This pine was definitely not dry; and even when it's dry, pine doesn't provide much heat. At the time, all of the trees of any size on our property were white pines. We tried for over an hour, but the wood would not ignite. Fortunately, Mom refused Ted's suggestion that we try gasoline.

Hence, I'm alive to tell this story!

Those first three winters in New Hampshire, we burned anything we could get our hands on. However, we did not sink to the level of the pilgrims in the movie "Exodus," who burned the seats inside their airliner because they were cold. But we came close.

Some of our neighbors heard of our plight and assisted with donations of firewood, but we still ran short. Even on a good day, you could see your breath inside the house.

When it was really cold Mom kept us home on weekends. She wouldn't let us bail out to a friend's house --it would have been too humiliating an admission. And it would be unfair if only one child had the opportunity to be warm.

That first winter, we learned about layering before it was a fashion statement. We always had to remove an outer shirt and socks when we went to school, otherwise we'd roast like marshmallows in the classroom. At night, we wore full sets of long underwear, wool socks, and hats to cover our ears when we went to bed. On those same days, we wore our coats inside the house. We sat huddled around the stove heat vent in between the dining and living rooms.

"Why did we leave Brooklyn?" one of my sisters wailed.

Ted snarled, "So that you wouldn't get raped! Now, shut up!" Rather than listen to the complaints, he stomped off upstairs to sit in an ice-cold bedroom. We froze in silence.

In the fall of 1958, our neighbor, Wilbur Burleigh, told us to lay pine boughs up against the exposed field stone foundation. When the snow blew in from the north, it would hit the boughs, freeze, and become an insulation layer and an external wind block. This stabilized the temperature in the basement and kept the floor from being ice-cold.

In the meantime, Dad was still in the Navy, at a base in Spain. Off watch, he was on the beach drinking wine. My mother was not amused!

Dad retired from the Navy in the summer of 1959. By winter, he was earning a civilian salary and we were able to finally heat the house with oil. No longer were we forced to waddle around the house wearing three layers of clothes, looking like a flock of multicolored penguins. Still, on really cold and windy days, we would fire up the furnace as a booster heat source.

January 1959. Our garden had failed again. Despite some of our neighbors sharing extra vegetables with us, food was tight. Mom was a great cook, but if you don't have enough ingredients, meals become sparse and repetitive. One night, she announced grandly, "Tonight we're having a French country meal, quiche lorraine with bacon!"

How many nights in a row can you eat quiche as the main entrée? As many as you have to when there's nothing else to eat.

Twenty years later in 1979, I was cooking at the Isaac Dow House in Newington, New Hampshire. I was informed that a quiche was part of the daily menu. I must have visibly gagged because the head chef asked me if I was all right. Choking back the bile, I replied, "I'm fine; I had a bad quiche once."

During those first years we became well acquainted with the county's U.S. Department of Agriculture's Surplus Food Program. Overall, the food provided was pretty good.

The best? Five-pound cans of peanut butter. When it was opened, there was at least two inches of crystal clear pure peanut oil on the top. It took powerful arms to mix the oil back into the solids to make it spreadable. I was a shrimpy kid and only got the job once. I didn't have powerful arms. As I cranked my skinny arm, some oil slopped out and ran down the side of the can. I lost control of the slippery can and it flipped. There was oil everywhere. One of my sisters started to cry and beat on me.

"We're going to starve!"

"Oh Michael," Mom said, and prevented me from being further pummeled.

Fifty years later I still cannot eat a peanut butter sandwich unless it has jam or something on it.

And those five-pound blocks of American cheese. It actually tasted pretty good when it was fresh. However, after about a week it tended to lose its flavor and became, in essence "food, rubber, yellow."

The worst offerings were the powdered milk and eggs. To this day, I view both of them with revulsion. Nor will I eat scrambled eggs at a breakfast buffet.

At the church after Dad's funeral in 2015, one of our neighbors pulled me aside.

"You know Mike, there was considerable doubt among the people in town that you folks were going to make it."

Virginia, Ted, Michael, and his sisters

But now that we had protein, we needed vegetables. And we had a lot to learn. But here's a question for the reader. What is your first New Hampshire harvest? Rock! After the soil is turned with a plow and broken up with a harrow, the rocks must be removed.

Our steel rake was taller than I was. Since I was the smallest and closest to the ground, my job was to pick up the broken pieces of shale and granite that were too fine for the rake. I remember one Sunday afternoon, 45 minutes after church services. I was in the dirt with sweat in my eyes, on "all fours," picking up rocks in 85-degree heat. I contemplated the biblical concept of "Sunday being the day of rest."

That may have something to do with my latter-day aversion to organized religion and love of supermarkets!

That first spring, Mom cried after the woodchucks ate an entire row of beans. Firearms weren't an option because someone would have to sit in the sun all day with a rifle. Instead, we deployed an alternative countermeasure. That April, Dad came home with a "secret weapon." He opened his coat. A little head popped out and looked around. Dad handed him to me. My face was promptly licked all over.

Mom was not a big fan of dogs but made an exception. She named him Gorgeous George after the wrestler. He was a border collie mix puppy, smart, fun, gregarious, and charming. He was a handsome tawny fellow, with a white chest bib with a black fur tipped ruff and upright black tipped ears.

Mom loved him for the same reason that the swiftest, the surviving, members of the local woodchuck population hated him. He was a ground-bound-avenging-eagle. With masterful skill and aplomb, he controlled, in actuality, eliminated, the chuck population in a quarter mile radius on all sides of the house.

However, he scrupulously avoided the yard of mom's best friend, Harriet Burleigh. It seems that he had cruised into Harriet's yard to snatch a chuck at the same time that she arrived with her 16 gauge. Suffice to say that after watching her dispatch the chuck in question, George never set foot on her property again.

With the chucks gone, what next? The bugs, worms, and fungi were still conspiring to starve us to death. Virginia was not known for half measures. Armed with the latest newfangled pesticide, she laid waste to the infestations. When DDT was banned, she cursed the U.S. government, but that is another story.

After a few years, we finally figured out how to raise enough food to feed ourselves. We ended up with two gardens, one 100 x 40 feet, the other 200 x 30 feet. We raised string beans, pole beans, wax beans, peas, okra, cucumbers, squash, tomatoes, peppers, sweet potatoes, zucchini, cantaloupes, honeydew, watermelons, corn, carrots, onions, lettuce, cabbage, and potatoes. The harvest was bountiful. Mom pickled, canned, and froze some of everything.

In the summer of 1960, Dad and Ted grew 1200 pounds of potatoes. I dug them. If you have never dug half a ton of potatoes by hand, take my advice, don't. Refer to my previous note about my love of supermarkets!

"Mom, what we were going to do with all these potatoes?"

"Remember how hungry we were two winters ago? Other people need help too."

We gave potatoes to anyone who was short or who had helped us through the previous winters.

One of our neighbors came back for more, saying, "the family likes them better than mine. Mine don't crunch like yours when you eat them. Mother says yours don't get mushy when you boil them either. Harold, these potatoes are some damn fine."

Dad smiled and gave him a 40-pound burlap sack full. We kept 400 pounds for ourselves. Then we donated 600 pounds of potatoes to the town food pantry. It was the largest donation they had ever received. After hearing about the size of the gift, Bud and Betsy Booth of Green Dream Farm slaughtered and donated one of their Guernsey's to the pantry. Bud explained, "People can't eat just potatoes."

Thanksgiving of 1960 was one for the ages. Any vegetable that you could name came from our garden and was on our plates. Add to that one 30-pound turkey with cornbread stuffing. Glorious!

From these experiences I absorbed some principles that guided me later in life.

- If you work at something long enough, you will be rewarded.

- Do not be ashamed or too proud to ask for help when you need it.

- There is no excuse for failing to help someone in their time of need. If it costs you a few bucks? So what? That's what money's for.

Thanks, Mom and Dad.

Brooklyn Alley Cat Mk1

Nowadays, "free range cats" in rural New Hampshire are slotted in as "snacks" in the non-domestic animal food chain, but in 1957, not so much.

Scrappy was a 13-pound gray and black tiger striped alley cat. My brother Ted found him when he was only a little bigger than a kitten. He decided that we were "cool enough to own him". We had no idea where he went or what he did when we let him out. We do know that on occasion he would arrive somewhat the worse for wear: "Hey, where'd the top third of his right ear go?"

He was willing to be playful and do cute "cat things." He didn't so much purr as make a sound like an unoiled ratchet. However, when he was bored with you, he would deliver a forehand swat with his claws retracted. If as we usually did, you persisted, you got the "rake" the paw with claws extended.

Complaints to Mom fell on deaf ears. "He swatted you once, right?"

When we were getting ready to move to New Hampshire, we fully intended to bring him with us. For that to happen, Scrappy would "have to be in the area" when it was time for us to leave. This was a subject of great consternation to my sisters. They were afraid that he'd be left behind. Fortunately, he was present and accounted for when we left Brooklyn.

What does a Brooklyn alley cat do when he arrives in the country? He had fought city rats and stray dogs, so fear was not a dominant component of his character. As any healthy tomcat would do, he ranged far and wide in his new world. His exploratory efforts were rewarded. Just a quarter mile down the hill, he discovered…PUSSY!

In fact, he discovered an entire population of lady cats living in a dairy barn. The local tomcats were simply no match for 13 pounds of "horny urban mean." Scrappy ran them off. They moved across the street to Kelsey's farm. The owner there wondered, "Where the hell did all these tomcats come from?"

"Brooklyn Alley Cat Mark 1" integrated the neighborhood in his way. Most of the local barn cats were various combinations of black and white. Several months after Scrappy moved to the Hook Road, this formerly dominant coloration became interlaced with gray and black tiger stripes. His offspring were slimmer and wirier than their ancestors as well. We didn't see much of Scrappy after he established his harem. When he did come home, it was to sleep. His bloodline lasted for close to 20 years.

Even the farmer down the hill laughed about it. "When your cat comes down to the barn, the other tomcats run away."

Going to Farnham's on the Lower Square

The Mars landing continued…

"We won the war. Now watch us build!"

Dover, New Hampshire in August 1957 was a thriving commercial hub. It was a magnet for people wishing to shop and work was plentiful. Factories were running at full tilt, some on three shifts. Others ran two shifts plus overtime. This was the industrial rolling thunder of small post-war American cities.

Central Avenue is Dover's main thoroughfare. It bisects the city on a north-south axis. Like most New Hampshire roads, it goes wherever it wants before delivering you to your destination. With the northbound one-way loop added to its eastern side, it looked kind of like a pregnant snake climbing over a rock.

From the south, visualize the lowercase letter "b." Extend the vertical line of the letter at both ends and kink them to the left. Situated inside and around the right-hand bulge were the industries that called the city "home" and fed and clothed it.

At the bottom of the "b" bulge, Eastern Air Devices pneumatically snorted and growled. Across the street, another factory was topped with its name "CLAROSTAT." When the sign was powered up at night, the smell of ozone razored your sinuses as huge blue and white neon letters demonically hummed, crackled, and spat high voltage illumination.

Then the road took a 90-degree-left hand uphill turn around a telephone pole. This brought you past the long four- to five-story expanse of Miller Shoe Company on the left. The pungent scent of worked leather punched your nostrils like a fist.

Cresting the hill, the rude boys of Miller, high school dropouts mostly, were humping hides into the maw of the building. They wore crew cuts, their taut muscles tucked into tight t-shirts. Boxes of "Luckys" were rolled up in most sleeves, cigarettes dangling from their lips, a la James Dean. They stared with overt hostility at the traffic crawling past. They were free to make any gesture or say whatever they wanted. You both knew that you weren't going to stop.

At the foot of the Upper Square, across the street to the right, was a small shopping plaza which housed a local institution. If you wanted groceries, Janetos Market and Butcher Shop would handle your needs. If you decided to go to the Lower Square, you took the left and drove around the Montgomery Ward appliance showroom. There the washing machines and stoves were fanned out in a semicircle facing the street, like a line of gleaming white battle tanks.

Did you want to go to the movies? You went straight. Depending on what was playing, you took a left to go to the Strand or a right to the Uptown. At this juncture, the aroma emanating from the loaves pumping out of the M&M bakery blew across the railroad tracks down 3rd Street to overwhelm the scent of leather.

There were no malls. The business district on both sides of Central Avenue was teeming. The Upper and Lower Squares were packed with storefronts, Hooz Ladies Clothing, JJ Newberrys, Rivers Camera, Western Auto and Harvey's Bakery. Everything had its own specialty store: shoes, jewelry, pianos, furniture, optometrists and sporting goods. On a Friday afternoon, you were hard pressed to find a parking space.

Being new to the area, with four children to clothe for the upcoming school year, Mom asked our neighbor, Mildred Haendler for advice. She told Mom that there was a clothing store in Dover that sold high quality clothing at reasonable prices.

"The Farnhams are the nicest people. You should take the children there for school clothes. If you tell me when you're going, I'll call ahead for you."

In the Fifties, country families were very conscious about how they presented themselves when they went out in public. You did not go into town unless you were properly dressed in "clean clothes with no holes." Visiting a clothing store imposed a special requirement. You respected the merchant and his wares. It would be unseemly not to have bathed and then try on clothing that someone else might buy later.

The day before our first visit to Dover, Mom started her preparations. In the afternoon, she washed all of our "town clothes" and hung them out to dry on the clothesline. That night, she heated the straightening combs on the kitchen stove and straightened my sisters' hair. Dad gave Ted and me haircuts. It was "old school", a pair of scissors and a comb. For me to sit still for 10 minutes was almost impossible back then. After several whacks upside of my head to still the beast, he was finished.

It was a clear, hot Friday in August 1957 about 3:00 PM. But not overly hot; the heat had broken earlier in the day. Dad eased the '49 Mercury Flathead V8 Coupe into an angled parking space. It was right in front of Farnhams' clothing store on the Lower Square just before the bridge. I was the smallest, so I sat in the front between my parents.

Dad told me, "Michael get out on the side with your mother." He climbed out the driver's side and locked the door. He came around the front of the car and deployed us.

He spoke crisply to my brother. "Ted, step up on the sidewalk! Michael stay right here by the door. Girls stay with your mother."

He walked around the side of the car, checking to make sure that the windows were shut and that the door and trunk locked. I didn't know it until I was an adult, but stated in combat terms, Dad was "clearing his six o'clock."

"Dad?" Ted looked back over his shoulder.

"Yes, Ted, right there. That's good."

Then, as Mom later recounted, "Traffic came to a screeching halt."

It was dead silent for a moment as the drivers processed what they were seeing. The store manager, a tall, bald, whiplike man, hurried out, "You must be the Wards!"

Finally, traffic began to roll again, albeit more slowly. Then a voice bellowed, "Hey look! Some niggers!"

Dad pivoted to face the source of the threat. The car was on the outer lane from where he stood. "You son of a bitch."

His rage was apparent and all but guaranteed that anyone exiting that car was going to be "well employed" for several minutes. The store manager was surprisingly fast. He sprinted out and caught Dad by the arm. "This is my town; I'll handle this."

He strode out into the street and pointed at the car. As he moved towards it, the driver must have sensed trouble. He grabbed the gear shift, slid it into first, goosed it, and the car scuttled away. Then the manager did a surprising thing. He ran down the street after the car. He was breathing hard when he came back up the street.

"He isn't going to get away with that. We don't treat people like that here. But I got his plate number. I got his plate. They'll be hearing from the police."

Meanwhile, a steady stream of people moved to and fro on the sidewalk. For the most part, they looked at us curiously.

A man in a yellow shirt walking by smiled and said, "Good afternoon. Where are you folks from?"

"We live in Lee," replied Dad coolly.

"I live over in Rollinsford. Glad you folks are here." He shook Dad's hand and went on his way.

A woman, well-dressed in a pastel blue suit, her dark hair styled in a bouffant, was wearing a faux pearl necklace and pill box hat and carried a clutch purse. She voiced a very different point of view. She glared at us and muttered under her breath, "Trash."

It was just loud enough for Mom to hear. She stepped up on the sidewalk and stared back at her with the superior level of ferocity that only a woman raised in Atlantic City and Brooklyn can deliver. The woman flushed from the intensity of her gaze. Thus silenced, she continued on her way.

A break appeared in the sidewalk traffic.

The store manager waved us over to the door. "Come on, let's get out of this heat into my store. We've got air conditioning!"

"Ted, don't let anyone within six feet of your mother, sisters, or brother. Go on, 'Gin."

Mom led the flying wedge formation. The manager held up his hand like a traffic cop. He blocked people coming up the sidewalk on the left. Ted stood with his arms extended straight out from his sides, fencing off folks coming down the street from the right.

As a unit, we moved into the store. Dad walked backwards into the store, taking up station as the rear guard. His head was pivoting like a turret as he stared down anyone thinking about getting too close.

Once inside the manager said, "I didn't recognize the car. They must be some out of town third-shift people. They aren't real Dover people. We aren't like that… I'm very sorry about that, Mr. and Mrs. Ward."

Then he turned to Dad and asked, "Are you a veteran?"

"Yes, U.S. Navy active duty."

"Well, I served too. I'm sorry and I apologize."

Smoothly and as gracefully as always, Mom interceded. "We understand that it's hard for some people here."

We're Going to Texas

This is one of the few stories in "Sketches" that is not connected to our life in Lee. But it is crucial to understanding who my father was. It happened long ago, during a time in America when nothing was guaranteed, and self-sacrifice was ennobling.

The Mess Attendants

It was a surreal apparition: a reddish-orange orb hanging silently in the night sky, slowly enlarging, then with increasing rapidity, expanding and descending. A demon fireball from hell.

A year before that fireball, in 1941, two U.S. Navy Mess Attendants (MAtts) were off watch, sitting on their bunks on the heavy cruiser, the USS San Francisco (CA-38). The older of the two was MAtt1c (First Class) Leonard R. Harmon, a big 6'4" 24-year-old farm boy from Cuero, Texas. He was a former high school athlete, but a heart murmur had initially prevented him from enlisting. However, he persisted, and he was accepted on his second attempt. Harmon was the steward of CA-38's Executive Officer, Commander Mark Crouter.

"Ward, when this is over, we're going to Texas. I'll take you out to the farm. I'll show you how life is meant to be lived. Forget about all that crap in Atlantic City. I'll even teach you to ride a horse!"

"You know, Harmon, that sounds pretty good," replied his 19-year-old companion, MAtt3c (Third Class) Harold Ward.

Harold E. Ward 1942

A Childhood in Exile

Ward was a 5'11", 140-pound wired bundle of trouble from Atlantic City. He was born in 1921 when his mother was 15 years old. She and her family were "light, bright, and damn near white." Harold began his life with two strikes against him: he was illegitimate, and his father was a seventeen-year-old "coal black nigger." He was summarily deemed to be "unfit", and he was "run off".

A Negro's social standing in the first half of the 20th century was based in large part on his or her complexion. Lighter skin equaled higher social standing. If you were light enough to "pass" for being white, you avoided contact with your darker-skinned brethren. If an individual or family were to be labeled as "Colored" or "Negro," discrimination was assured.

The existence of a brown-skinned child in a lily-white family of upper-class Negroes was an embarrassment that could not be tolerated. Harold was sent away to live with his grandparents in the New Jersey countryside. He was 10 years old when his mother died from tuberculosis. About a year later, his step-grandfather had a stroke. The Depression was crushing the country. His grandmother could not support him and her own children. His other relatives of adequate means in New York City viewed him as trouble and put him out. They shuffled him among his nine aunts and uncles in the city like a hot rock handed off to a sucker. In one instance, he was set out on the curb in the morning to be picked up with the trash. He depended on "anyone who would take him in."

Unfortunately, the worst was yet to come. In 1933, he was exiled to his aunts in Atlantic City. There, the remainder of his childhood was spent in Dickensian squalor, shuffling between the poorest and most disreputable of his relatives. A stable living arrangement and regular meals were foreign to him. A life where he was not viewed as a burden seemed unobtainable. His existence was reduced to the simplest possible terms, endure or perish.

One aunt who owned a rooming house/brothel, tired of his antics and punted him to another aunt. If living in a rooming house with prostitutes was horrible, living in an apartment with two of them was worse. This aunt and her female lover were two extraordinarily homely prostitutes.

"They made me work because they weren't very successful," Harold recalled in 2015.

As a junior high schooler, he supported himself, his aunt, her lover, and two cousins. Every morning before school at 4:00 AM, he stood in the "shape up" line at the local dairy. If he was picked by the super, he would earn 50 cents a day as a milk wagon helper. He kept 5 cents for himself and gave his aunt the rest to feed the household. When the milk wagon drivers stopped at a diner for their breakfast, Harold wasn't allowed inside. If a driver was kind, he'd bring him out a donut. If not, he didn't eat. If he wasn't picked and came home without the 45 cents, he was beaten. His 8th grade teacher, Miss Alice Banton, bought him a suit for graduation because he was destitute.

"Join the Navy and See the World"

In 1939, Harold graduated from Atlantic City Technical High School as an electrician's apprentice. He joined the U.S. Navy as his path to escape the squalor of his youth. There his independence could be established; and he was embarking on a career that would enable him to see the world. No one told him that his apprenticeship was useless in the U.S. Navy. Once he enlisted, his dream was erased.

One of Woodrow Wilson's first official acts as President after taking office in 1913 was to segregate the armed forces. He justified it under the assumption that Negroes were mentally inferior, cowardly and incapable of following orders. This was an early 20th-century reality despite a history of blacks' service to this country dating back to the Revolution. In December 1775, George Washington wrote a letter to Colonel Henry Lee stating that "Success in the war would come to whatever side could arm the blacks fastest."

Wilson's action came on top of an executive order signed in 1901 by President McKinley. The order allowed the U.S. Navy to recruit 500 Filipinos per year to serve as Mess Attendant-Stewards. Upon completion of their three-year enlistment, they would be granted U.S. citizenship.

The Naval Officer Corps had always had stewards to tend to their personal needs. Stewards cooked and served officers' meals in the wardroom. They also made their beds and washed, pressed, and set their uniforms. Decorations, belt buckles, and shoes had to be impeccably polished. Woe to the steward whose uniform preparation failed to meet the inspection standards of his officer. In short, they were servants.

The personnel demands caused by the expansion of the Navy in the 1930s outstripped the number of available Filipinos. It was decided that "Negroes" would take their place as Mess Attendant-Stewards. This became immediately problematic. The Filipinos regarded Negroes as uncultured animals and treated them as such. The Negroes resented being lumped in with and then ordered around by "non-citizens", some with limited English-speaking skills.

Years later, Harold reflected on this. "Since the Filipinos had been in service longer than us, they all held higher ranks. They were bastards and treated us like crap. We had one Chief Steward removed though.

"Since we weren't enlisted personnel, the Navy didn't allow us to eat in the enlisted mess. So, we ate our meals in the wardroom after the officers finished. We were supposed to eat the same food as the officers. We paid into a pool for our food out of a monthly stipend. The Chief Steward was pocketing our stipends and feeding us the cheapest and worst food he could get. Meanwhile, he and the other Filipino stewards were eating what the officers ate. Finally, we had enough.

One evening, Leonard Harmon, slid a plate of what we were being fed in front of Commander Crouter.

"'What the hell is this?'

"'Canned salmon and rice.' replied Harmon.

"'Is this what they are serving in the wardroom tonight?'

"'No sir, this is what the Chief Steward is feeding the Mess Attendants.'

"Crouter blew up. 'I wouldn't feed this crap to my cat. Get this garbage out of here and send him up to my office.'"

"The Chief Steward was transferred from a heavy cruiser to a destroyer escort. His replacement was also a Filipino, but he'd learned from his predecessor's mistake. He'd write us up whenever he could, but we'd made our point. To this day, I won't eat canned salmon."

Harold had successfully completed segregated boot camp, meeting the same standards as white sailors. However, instead of being a Seamen 1st Class, black sailors became Mess Attendants Third Class, an unrated position as employees of the U.S. Navy. There was no process in place for them to become enlisted men with rank. They were paid less than Seamen 1st, but still subject to the Universal Code of Military Justice. Touching a weapon or ammunition or speaking to a member of the press would result in a court martial.

The Navy was confounded. The Filipino stewards had been obedient and docile. The Negroes, especially the better educated ones from the North, could be downright hostile. Putting it mildly, race relations in the U.S. Navy were tense.

Harold did not respond well in this environment. On CA-38 he and the officers he was detailed to serve shared one commonality: they hated each other. His repeated insubordination and hostility resulted in his being summoned to Commander Crouter's office.

"Ward, I don't write the policies, but it's my job to enforce them," the Exec explained. "We both know that they are unfair, but neither of us can do a damn thing about it. I'm sorry, but you're just going to have to live through it."

Things came to a head when his assigned officer, a Marine 2nd Lieutenant from South Carolina, deemed the laundering of his socks to be sub-standard. He cursed Harold out and slapped his face. Harold exploded. He picked up a bayonet and chased the Marine out of the wardroom and up two decks before he was tackled by a pair of Mess Attendants.

Years later, Harold recalled, "I have never seen a Marine run so fast in my life!"

There are no circumstances that warrant an officer cursing an enlisted man. To strike one is a court martial offense. To defuse the situation, the Marine was taken off the ship in less than 24 hours. However, no matter what infraction an officer may have committed, enlisted men cannot chase officers through a warship with a 10-inch bayonet. Consequently, Harold was confined to quarters, and his pay was cut for a month. He was spared a court martial because officers were responsible for the laundering of their own underclothing and socks.

The officers resented the fact that he wasn't sent to the brig. It was agreed that his attitude lacked the proper level of respect and deference. He needed to have his perspective adjusted. He was brought up on charges, and a "Captain's Mast" was convened.

"What charge has caused this sailor to be brought before this court?" Commander Crouter inquired.

"Mess Attendant 3rd Class Ward has repeatedly exhibited 'silent contempt' of and to the officers in the wardroom," replied the charging officer.

"I can find no such charge anywhere in the Universal Code of Military Justice. Nor do I know how one could effectively prove such. The charge is dismissed."

"But Sir!"

"This court is now closed."

The officers were furious. This could not stand. Harold was deemed "unfit to serve the officers and gentlemen of the U.S. Navy." He was banished from the wardroom. His new billet was cleaning toilets.

"I became 'King of the Heads.' But I didn't care. Anything was better than waiting on those sons of bitches," related Ward.

After this incident, Leonard Harmon stepped in and became Harold's surrogate "big brother." He knew the system, helped Harold out of further jams and kept him straight. Harold was really looking forward to a new start in Texas when his enlistment was up.

A Day That Will Live in Infamy

"When the Japanese attacked Pearl Harbor on December 7th, we were arrogant, we were unprepared, and we paid for it." In 2015, that morning was still vivid in Harold's mind. "But personally, I had no quarrel with the Japanese. I had never thought much about them. All I wanted to do was to get the hell out of the Navy when my enlistment was up.

"It was unreal. From my lookout perch on the San Francisco, I watched them fly right over my head. I knew they were Japanese because they had giant meatballs on their wings. They looked close enough to touch. I could see the pilots making adjustments in their cockpits. They flew right down Battleship Row like it was a movie. Their precision was simply incredible. Each pilot knew his designated route and target. I called down my report to the Officer of the Deck (OOD).

"Sir, Battleship Row is under attack by Japanese naval aircraft. Several ships are on fire and one has exploded.

"The OOD was furious. 'Ward, I don't need any of this crap from you. Consider yourself on report and confined to your quarters when you get off watch.'

"A minute later, a white sailor ran down to the OOD's watch station and confirmed the attack. We immediately went to our battle stations.

"But they ignored us. We were in a dry dock across the harbor, undergoing an overhaul. The ship was in pieces. We had no guns. All of our turrets were on shore being overhauled in the armory. We were defenseless.

"Some fool came out on deck with a .45 and started shooting at a Japanese plane. A bunch of guys tackled him and took away his pistol. They were afraid that if a Japanese pilot saw him, they would retaliate. With no major armaments, we'd be a sitting duck. They dragged the sailor below deck and beat the crap out of him. The Bosun's Mate threw him in the brig to keep him from being killed.

"I grew up as an orphan without many friends. I stood and watched as some of the few that I had made in the Navy evaporated. Their ships burned, exploded, burned some more, and sank. If that didn't kill them and they jumped into the bay, the burning fuel in the water got them.

"The Japanese took from me. The U.S. Navy was no longer my enemy; the Japanese were. I was a sailor, and we were at war."

Harold survived Pearl Harbor.

13 November 1942, sometime after 0124 (UTC+11), off the north coast of Guadalcanal

Task Group 67.4 had been detailed to support the U.S. reinforcement of Guadalcanal.

The previous afternoon, an out-of-control Japanese torpedo bomber crashed into the stern of CA-38. The subsequent explosion in the aft Battle Two station started an intense fire. Fifteen men were killed and another 29 were wounded. Cmdr. Crouter was trapped in Battle Two and was seriously burned.

Cmdr. Crouter refused medical evacuation. "I'm of no use in a hospital bed. If I stay on board, I can help fight the ship."

Harmon waved off the ship's medics and personally tended the Commander's burns all night.

A discussion ensued among the task group command staff as to whether the Japanese pilot whose plane had crashed into the stern should receive a military burial. This was before the era of Kamikaze attacks. The idea was abandoned when it was realized that it would damage crew morale. And since the whereabouts of the Japanese fleet was unknown, CA-38 could not risk being caught in the middle of a sea burial of 15 men. The dead were prepared and stored in the meat locker until such time as they could be safely interred.

In the meantime, the Japanese withdrew from the area and thought the U.S. had as well. They had not. Now, less than 12 hours later, they and the U.S. Navy were about to engage in the "3rd Battle of Savo Island," or the "Sea Battle of Guadalcanal."

The Japanese were attempting to reinforce their garrison on Guadalcanal. If successful, they could then take control of the island. From that vantage point, they would attack and invade Australia, only 800 miles away. The Allies had no viable assets available to stop their invasion.

The Japanese staged a nighttime infantry landing and provisioned their guns for a shore bombardment, not ship to ship combat. That type of ordinance was designed to explode on contact and spread shrapnel over a broad area like a shotgun. Armor-piercing shells do the exact opposite, they penetrate a ship's steel armor plating and explode. When the fighting began, the Japanese fleet had their armor-piercing shells stowed below in the magazines. It took time to swap out shells weighing 1,400 pounds each. The Japanese had no time, and it cost them dearly.

The Japanese flag was carried by the Hiei. She had been designed by a British naval architect in 1913 as a heavy cruiser. Since then, she had been refitted as a Kongo class battleship. Her primary armament was 8-14" guns, with a throw weight of 11,920 pounds per broadside. The Japanese Navy did not have radar. Instead, they relied on a highly sophisticated optics system for nighttime operations. The refit had left her lighter cruiser armor in place, giving her a top speed of 35 knots.

The American flagship, CA-38, was a nine-year-old New Orleans class heavy cruiser. In terms of primary armament, her 9-8" guns had a broadside throw weight of 2,340 pounds, almost a five-ton disadvantage. She had been retrofitted with GE's state-of-the art SG25 radar. Her top speed was 38 knots.

Two of the U.S. Navy's new Benson class destroyers equipped with the SG25 were in the task group's lead element. In their case, it was a built-in feature, not a retrofit. Their captains and crews had been extensively trained in its operation since day one. In contrast, the Task Group Commander Rear Admiral Daniel J. Callaghan and CA-38's

Captain Cassin Young had no operational training with its use. In fact, the Admiral had been on the ship for 15 days, and the Captain had transferred onboard less than 24 hours before.

The U.S. Navy was initiating an engagement that they could not afford to lose. They were outnumbered, 17 to 13, and outgunned by the opposition's battleships and heavy cruisers. In pitch darkness Task Group 67.4 surprised the Japanese. They drove into the center of the resupply fleet at 25 knots, disrupting the invasion. A vicious close-range battle with long-range weapons then ensued.

Harold recalled, "We were making 25 knots, and we steamed right into a mess. We were in the middle of this terrible exchange of fire from three points... shells are hitting us and the guns are constantly firing, and the ship is shaking and shuddering... all of a sudden - BANG - I go flying off the ladder and I wind up on my back on the deck. It was a nasty, nasty scrap.

"It's not like the movies or TV or whatever. You're not sitting around thinking 'what am I gonna do?' and 'am I gonna die?' and 'blah blah blah.' All you're thinking is 'Christ I hope they don't sink this son of a bitch because I can't get outta here!' You hope your gunnery and your maneuvers are proper so you can get the hell outta there... without having to swim."

CA-38 was taking heavy fire from Hiei's sister ship, the Kirishima, 4,000 yards away. Admiral Callaghan did not trust what he couldn't see. He ignored the radar reports of contacts outside of his visual range. Instead, the command and control of his weapons was optical and reactive. They fired at muzzle flashes aimed in their direction.

In the meantime, the light cruiser USS Atlanta had been ahead of them in the column. She had been triangulated in a barrage from three Japanese destroyers. She was heavily damaged and had no functioning power or radio. She drifted backwards, a blacked-out hulk, into the slot between the two ships. CA-38 never saw her. Atlanta was shredded with two salvoes of 9-8" shells intended for the Kirishima. Admiral Norman Scott was killed in the exchange. The USS Atlanta was scuttled the next afternoon.

The Hiei and the American destroyer Laffey (DD459) were on a collision course. Their combined closing speed was more than 40 knots. Just before impact, the Laffey pivoted around the bow of the Hiei. With only 20 feet of separation, the Laffey ran down her side. They raked the flagship's superstructure and bridge with 4-5" and 20 and 40 mm antiaircraft guns. The Hiei's guns could not be depressed sufficiently to defend herself. She took a pounding. The point-blank blows to the flag bridge wounded Vice Admiral Abe, the task force commander, and killed his Chief of Staff Captain Suzuki.

The Laffey's gun run had changed the course of history, by disrupting the command and control of the Japanese fleet. Clear of the Hiei's flanks, the USS Laffey died. Once exposed, her remaining 3-5" guns were no match for the triangulated firepower of two battleships and two destroyers. She exploded as the order to abandon ship was passed. Of her crew of 247, 59 were killed and 116 wounded.

At the same time, the Hiei continued to take a beating as other American destroyers duplicated the Laffey's attack. Her steering gear was disabled by shells from CA-38 and locked into a right-hand turn. No longer combat capable, the remaining command staff evacuated. The next day she was mortally wounded by U.S. Navy TBF torpedo bombers. Her engine compartment flooded, and Japanese destroyers then scuttled her with torpedoes.

CA-38 did not fare much better. In less than 45 minutes, she took 45 large caliber hits. Twenty-five of those were from the Hiei's 14" guns. Commander Crouter was killed when one of them tore through his cabin. Just after the Laffey's attack, from less than 3,000 yards, the Hiei scored a direct hit on the flag bridge. Admiral Daniel J. Callaghan, Captain Cassin Young, and the rest of the Task Group Command staff save one officer were killed. Had armor piercing ordinance been used, the bridge would have been torn off, and the ship possibly sunk.

Led by Pharmacist's Mate Lynford Bondsteel, Leonard Harmon and Harold went out on deck amidships to recover casualties. Harmon yelled, "I'll stay with Bondsteel. Ward, you get another stretcher." Harold turned and ran for the hatch. He undogged it and stepped through. Turning around, he looked up and saw the glow of an incoming round. It was going to be close.

Harmon screamed to Bondsteel, "Look out Doc!"

Harmon threw his body on top of Bondsteel. Harold finished dogging the hatch.

"The demon fireball from hell" landed, and the world ended. The 6" shell from the Hiei, less than 3,000 yards away, had impacted just outside the hatch Harold stood behind. The spall blew backward and seriously wounded Harmon. Bondsteel survived because Harmon had protected him. He, in turn, carried Harmon to the sickbay.

From the waist down, Ward was perforated with shrapnel. When he came to in the sick bay, it was dark and quiet. The emergency lighting died and then relit, the power fluctuating in response to battle damage. In the dim light, Ward saw that Harmon was strapped to the cot next to him. Several times he reached out to touch his friend, but with straps holding him back, it was too far. Several times over the next few hours, he called Harmon's name. "I could hear him breathing, but he never answered me."

The Cost of Freedom

In the end, at a horrendous cost for both sides, the U.S. Navy repelled the invasion. Vice Admiral Abe, not knowing the strength of his enemy and fearing the imminent arrival of a squadron of U.S. battleships, withdrew under cover of darkness. Had he waited until dawn to assess the situation, the Japanese would have won the battle and quite possibly the war. An enraged Admiral Yamamoto recalled him to

Tokyo and later forced him to resign. The Empire of the Rising Sun would expand no more.

On the other side, Task Group 67.4 had been reduced from 13 capital ships to a combat capable light cruiser and a destroyer. The remaining six ships, though underway, were no longer combat effective.

Just after 11:00 AM, CA-38 was steaming at 15 knots and down by the bow. I-25, a Japanese submarine, fired a spread of torpedoes at her. They missed and ran under her bow. One of the misses became a direct hit on the flank of the light cruiser USS Juneau. It exploded underneath her magazine. She went up in a 1,000-foot pyre. Since I-25's whereabouts were unknown, the remaining ships could not engage in rescue operations. Of the Juneau's 100 plus survivors in the water, ultimately, only 10 survived their wounds, drowning or shark attacks. The remainder of the ship's complement of 678 perished in the explosion. All five of the Sullivan brothers on the Juneau were lost when she died.

In the span of three days, over 1,700 U.S. sailors and 4,900 Japanese sailors and soldiers on transports died. So many ships were sunk—a total of 21 in the first day alone, that Savo Sound was nicknamed "Iron Bottom Sound."

In the only integrated task evolution by the U.S. Navy, MAtt1c Leonard R. Harmon (Navy Cross) and the Task Group Commander, Rear Adm. Daniel J. Callaghan (Medal of Honor) were piped over the side together. Two by two, another 90 of their brothers followed them into the Pacific.

In 2010, Harold said, "In the end, the color of your skin doesn't matter. In war, all blood runs red."

On July 25, 1943, the USS Harmon (DE-678) slid down the ways in Quincy, Massachusetts. It was the first capital ship of the U.S. Navy to be named for a Negro sailor.

Pharmacist's Mate Bondsteel received the Silver Star. Ward received a Purple Heart. In later years, he was told that he qualified for a Bronze Star. To which he replied, "What do I need a medal for? My body is full of it."

For the next 70 years, shrapnel from the engagement continued to work its way out of his body. In August 2014, he developed a hitch in his stride from a piece of dislodged shrapnel in his right knee. He would continue to limp from it until his passing on June 9, 2015.

Pharmacist's Mate Bondsteel sent Harold a Christmas card every year from 1945 until his passing around 2005.

In 1959, after 20 years of service, my father Harold E. Ward retired as a Commissaryman Petty Officer First Class. The Navy's back channel reference to his behavior on CA-38 effectively barred him from making Chief Petty Officer. Until the day he died, he cursed the United States Navy for not allowing him to fire a shot in anger during World War II.

In 2006, Harold looked back and remarked, "We never made it to Texas. When the war was over, all my close friends from high school and the Navy were dead."

In Appreciation

I extend my sincere thanks to the following individuals for their assistance in writing this story.

Mr. Tom Gibbs: Harold's Interviewer and Historian, National WWII Museum New Orleans, La.

Mr. Seth Paridon: Historian, National WWII Museum New Orleans, La.

Four-Tenths of a Mile

The definition of a patriot.
A man volunteering in the service of his country.
Accepting inconceivable sacrifices.

To defend
A place, not perfect
A place, capable of change
A place, where effort mattered
A place, where one could begin
A life
A family
A future.

Harold and Virginia Ward

I was 27 years old on a sunny January midafternoon in 1980. I walked into the kitchen of my parents' house on Lee Hook Road in Lee, New Hampshire.

Dad sat hunched over, stone silent, face drawn tight, elbows on his knees. His gaze was bore sighted at the kitchen floor three feet in front of him. His eyes reflected horrors that had escaped from the vault in his memory that protected him from the past. A glass of Jack Daniels was held with both hands to keep it from shaking.

"Hey Dad, how are you doing?"

"Not so good, Michael. I'm not right."

"What's wrong?"

"Ahhhhh… I don't want to talk about it." His hands shook as he spoke, slopping some Jack on the floor. "Damn…" He swore quietly. He straightened up, turned, and put his glass down on the kitchen table.

"Do you want a towel?"

Irritated and angered with his clumsiness, he waved me off. "No Michael, I'll get one." He stood slowly, looking much older than his 68 years. I looked at him and thought, "What the hell?" I walked past him into the living room.

Mom sat by a bench perched on a stool. She was a viper-like fury, quiet, lethal and hissing.

"Did you know him?"

"Who?"

"That asshole who shot himself."

"Uh yeah, but not well. He wasn't a friend."

"Why the hell didn't he do it in his town? Why did he have to do it here?"

Several Weeks Before

Harold had been on night patrol as a Lee policeman when he got the call. A young man had committed suicide at a friend's house. He triaged the scene and called an ambulance to collect the body. He then signed off watch. He knew what was coming next. He'd already lived through it in and after World War II. Now it was back, and he couldn't unsee it.

He had been a sailor in a wartime U.S. Navy that wouldn't let him man a weapon. His duty required him to recover casualties while under fire, exposed on the open deck of his warship. You can dodge a bullet. You cannot dodge 6-inch high explosive rounds or their shrapnel children.

His last battle on the USS San Francisco (CA-38), had taken the life of his best friend and almost his as well. Eventually, his body repaired itself. But every November 13th, he went back to a place beyond comprehension. A place where there was no certainty, where nothing he had ever learned or understood applied. It was into this void that he had fallen, but now his memories had escaped the night. They were crushing him in the daytime.

That day, Mom's disgust and rage were visceral; focused. "Look at him! He's been like that for three weeks. He won't even leave the house. He's right back to where he was when he came back from the war 35 years ago; screaming, thrashing, sweating, and crying nightmares. It took me 10 years to calm him down until he could sleep through the night. But every time a piece of shrapnel worked its way out of his body at night, they would start up again. Those goddamn wars never end."

It was more than three months before he returned to work as a policeman.

Arthur and Irene Pratte

"My Arthur is a hero," Irene Pratte said quietly, sadly, reverently.

It was the summer of 1959. I had been in our neighbor's, the Pratte's, living room on Lee Hook Road. I was a seven-year-old kid bursting with new-found knowledge. I said to Mrs. Pratte, "Mr. Haendler helped build the atom bomb and end the war!"

She looked at me for a few long seconds and then replied, "Mike, come upstairs with me. I want to show you something."

We went up the narrow staircase into her bedroom. She opened a wooden box on her dresser. Inside were medals. Some of them I recognized from studying Dad's 1940 U.S. Navy Bluejacket's Manual. A Silver Star, a Bronze Star, Purple Heart, and others I couldn't identify, were all living on a bed of shiny white silk.

She continued. "He wasn't the same when he came home. He enlisted with his high school classmates, his best friends. That's what boys did in America then; they all joined together. All five Sullivan brothers died when their ship was sunk in the Pacific. After that, why the Army would put everyone from the same town in the same unit is beyond me.

But they did." She looked down at the floor and shook her head in resignation.

She paused. "I know Helmut worked on the atom bomb and helped end the war. But he was in a lab. He didn't have to bury himself under his friend's bodies to escape the German bayonets when they overran his position. They killed the survivors, even those trying to surrender. After that Arthur fought the Germans like a madman.

"He was wounded so many times, I lost count. He can't take morphine for pain; it has no effect on him anymore. That's how he got all these medals. To this day, he hates anything German, including his next-door neighbor Helmut Haendler.

"But he's not the Arthur I knew and loved before the war. He was the handsomest, funniest, and sweetest boy in school. Now, he has a terrible temper and horrible screaming nightmares. It's awful watching and hearing your man suffer and not be able to do anything to help him. That's why he drinks. It's the only thing that calms him.

"I know Harold saw some awful things in the Navy. Have you ever heard his nightmares? Virginia told me that he has them. It's what happens to men if they live through combat. No one told us that our men would come home as strangers, wrecked. But he's my Arthur, and I love him. And I know Virginia loves Harold.

"There's just no comparison between doing experiments in a lab and being in combat. Hitler and the Nazis had to be stopped. My Arthur helped stop them."

Helmut and Mildred Haendler

Several weeks later, I was talking to Mildred Haendler in the living room of her house next door. "Michael, they had to be stopped. Everyone was afraid that they were going to take over the world. After Pearl Harbor, all the men signed up for the draft. It's what you did." She spoke with a quiet intensity.

"Helmut was a chemist; the government told him where to go. It wasn't like he could have joined the Marines if he'd wanted to. He came home and told me that he had been assigned to a top-secret project that would end the war. Then he said, 'But you need to know that we probably won't be able to have a family. The project will make me sterile.'

"We were living in New Jersey and he was working in a lab in New York City. He couldn't tell me what he was working on. Just that it was an incredibly powerful weapon on the edge of known science. He always kissed me goodbye in the morning. He told me that if there was an accident in the lab, I wouldn't be able to touch or see his body again because of the radiation. He also said if the accident was really bad, New York City and the surrounding area would instantaneously cease to exist.

"The stress on him was incredible. He would leave before sunrise and come back after dark. He had months, years of working 14- to 16-hour days. But no matter how late he came home, I always had his dinner waiting for him. And each night he went through the same ritual. After dinner, he'd pour himself a glass of brandy. Then he'd sit and stare at the wall, sipping that one glass of brandy without saying a word until 10 p.m. Then we'd go to bed."

She paused, and then she spoke about her man with the same steel-edged intensity as Virginia and Irene. It is a steel that I later came to understand and define as patriotism.

"The Germans and Japanese had to be stopped. They were going to take over the world and kill or enslave anyone that they didn't like. We had given up our dreams of a family to help save our country and the world. Our children, Blanca and Steven are a miracle.

"Arthur and Harold had terrible experiences in combat. I know they have nightmares, but for them it's over, they aren't going to die.

"Helmut was always a quiet man, but the project made him even quieter. He helped build a weapon that ended the war. At the same time, it opened Pandora's box. They created a weapon that in the wrong hands could wipe out mankind. This still haunts him, and it will for the rest of his life."

In the summer of 1959
The definition of a patriot
Was written and paid for by the wives
All living within four-tenths of a mile

On a dirt road
In Lee, New Hampshire
Population 400.

A Sirloin Steak

There are some special people in this world for whom righting a wrong is an innate behavior.

In the fall of 1941, my mother, Virginia White, enrolled at Temple University in Philadelphia, Pennsylvania. The school's health policy mandated that all students have annual dental examinations. She was referred by the school to a Colored dentist.

He was handsome, tall, light skinned, and impeccably dressed. He picked her up at school and drove her to his office in his new Chevrolet convertible.

"I'm sorry Miss White, but you have six rotted teeth. They can't be filled and will have to be extracted."

This was a surprise, since she had always brushed her teeth religiously. But having never seen a dentist before, she believed him. And, unfamiliar with second opinions, she consented to the extractions.

Turned out it was a big city scam perpetuated against young girls from the country who had never seen a dentist before. He made a fortune yanking teeth from Colored girls at Temple.

In the summer of 1958, the late Dr. Harry Chapman DDS, practicing in the old Masonic Temple on Locust Street in

Dover, New Hampshire, examined her remaining teeth. When he completed his exam, he was furious.

"Virginia, your uppers are the least likely candidates for rot. The fact that he took them sequentially from your upper jaw is because they were the easiest to extract. Your remaining teeth are beautiful. There is absolutely no evidence of rot in any of your remaining teeth.

"This is a crime, Virginia. It was only 17 years ago, so he's very likely still practicing. What was his name? I went to school with some fellows on the dentistry board in Philadelphia. When they hear about this, they'll revoke his license to practice."

"No, Dr. Chapman, it's done. I've got four children and Harold's at sea. I just don't have the time to go through with it."

Dr. Chapman was enraged. He shook his head and cursed under his breath. His wife, his hygienist, sat quietly. The color drained from her face. He asked her to order a plate for Mom.

"Dr. Chapman, I can't afford it."

"Virginia, I am offended and disgusted by what that 'son of a...'. He stopped because I was sitting there. I was only five years old at the time.

"…what that 'man' did to you. I can't even call him a dentist. This is an affront to my profession. It has to be made right. Don't worry about it. Pay me when you can."

The plate arrived several weeks later. On the way home from the office, Mom stopped to buy groceries at Marcotte's Market in Newmarket. Bill Crafts, the butcher, had once asked Mom why she never bought good steaks. She told him.

Today she said, "Bill! I got my plate!"

"Really, Virginia, I'm so happy for you! Let me find you something special." He was grinning from ear to ear as he went back to the meat locker.

That night, we kids had chuck steak. And as usual, we ate like wolves. Mom, on the other hand, ate slowly with her eyes closed. A smile adorned her face as she savored every bite.

In the late summer of 1958, Virginia Ward enjoyed her first sirloin steak since 1941.

The Ward family extends our sincerest thanks to the late Dr. Harry Chapman DDS and Mr. William "Bill" Crafts of Marcotte's Market, who, collectively, to borrow a quote from Star Trek, "made it so."

American Heroes

The advancement of civil rights in the United States was based in large part on the actions of normal people. These were individuals who did not stand idly by in the face of injustice. Individuals who, without fanfare, did the right thing, in the right place, at the right time.

The stories prefixed "American Hero" commemorate some of those individuals. Their heroism will never be forgotten. May their souls above be untroubled; may their sleep be sound. For the Ward family, the sun shines a bit brighter today because of their actions over 50 years ago.

American Hero: The Chemistry Teacher

For a first-year high school teacher, the handling of your classroom during an extraordinary event becomes the foundation upon which your reputation is based. In this case, no doubt was left in the minds of Roger Woodhead's students, peers, or the community as to where he stood.

I was hitchhiking home from school on a warm spring afternoon in 1969. I was a 16-year-old junior at Oyster River High School in Durham, New Hampshire. I stood at the intersection of Route 4 north and Route 155A west just outside of Durham. A burgundy 1969 Ford Mustang 302 V8 convertible rumbled to a stop. Grabbing the handle, I opened the door and climbed into the black leather bucket seat.

"Thanks, Mr. Woodhead!"

Roger Woodhead was the chemistry teacher at Oyster River High School from the early days of the school district in the late fifties until the eighties. As far as teachers go, he was known as being a good guy and a bit of a character.

"How's it going, Mike?"

"Okay."

"Say, Mike. Do you mind if I ask you a question?"

I hesitated for a second, then remembered what my older brother Ted had told me. "Mike, you can trust Mr. Woodhead. He's on our side. He's okay; he likes Colored people."

"Ummm, no."

"Do the other kids give you a hard time about your race?"

"Used to happen when new kids came into the district, but not much anymore."

"I'm glad to hear that. It was pretty tough for your brother, you know."

"I know, but he never talked much about it."

We rolled off down Route 155A towards Lee, heading west into the bright afternoon sunlight. He paused for a minute, parsing his thoughts.

"Back in 1959, I was in my first year at Oyster River. I had been teaching chemistry in Somersworth when the job opened up. Professionally, it was a big opportunity, so I went for it and got it. Anyway, there was a terrible incident in my classroom concerning your brother. Did he ever tell you about it?"

I looked at him curiously, "No."

"You were kind of young then; I can see why he didn't. Anyway, Ted sat in one of the front rows. He was a good student and a good kid. He minded his own business. He never bothered anyone else. A boy sitting in the back had been heaping muttered racial slurs on him during class for several weeks. He wasn't saying it loud enough for me to hear up front, but everyone else in the class could.

"I didn't know anything about it until two weeks later. One of the girls in the class finally told me what had been happening. It really upset me that I didn't know what was going on. I paid a lot more attention to my classroom chatter after that.

"So, one day, the boy said something clearly directed at Ted, utterly personal and totally foul. He said it so loudly that everyone, including me, could hear it. The classroom was dead silent. I have never been that angry in a class before or since. I was furious. But I had to control my temper. It was my first year. If I lost control, I'd lose the respect of my students. I couldn't allow that to happen. If I did, I'd be finished as a teacher. Somehow, I kept it in check.

"But his behavior couldn't go unpunished. Sending him to the office wouldn't do any good. There was nothing they could do that would have a lasting effect. So I made a decision. Your brother Ted was an athlete. He could handle himself, so I let him. I picked up my notes, turned around and went into the apparatus room behind the demonstration table in the front of the classroom.

"I was told that Ted got up, walked to the back of the room and delivered an uppercut straight into the motormouth. Then he returned to his seat and sat down. A couple of minutes later I returned and continued teaching. I didn't look at him or the other boy. Nor did I ask or make any comment about what happened while I was gone. No one in the class said a thing.

"The boy's face was a mess. He had blood all over his hands, face, and shirt. None of the girls would even lend him a handkerchief. He spent the rest of the class dripping blood with his hands covering his bleeding mouth. I just taught and ignored him. At the end of the period, his classmates, even those who didn't care about Ted, refused to speak to him or acknowledge his condition. He was silenced.

"I suppose I should have gone down to the office and reported it. I don't know why, but I just didn't. I guess it's because I saw how the Navy treated Colored men in the war. Your people have suffered long enough in this country. I wasn't going to put up with it, especially in my classroom.

"I was lucky that the room was empty for the next period. If not, there would have been hell to pay for all of us. I would have lost my job, and both boys would have been suspended. I kept the other boy after class. I didn't ask him what happened. I just said, 'Go to the nurse and get tended to. Then go see the janitor. He's not going to clean up your mess. You're going to do it. Ask him for cleaning supplies to wash your desk, the floor, and the wall. You will also have to pay to replace any textbooks with blood on them.'"

"To get to the school nurse's office, he had to walk through the entire school in a blood-soaked shirt. Everybody saw him, and no one said a word. The nurse didn't say anything about it either. Whenever a student is injured at school, a report must be filed and sent to the district office. The report states the nature, severity, and cause of the injury. It includes the names of the witnesses, when and where it occurred, and the measures taken to treat it. There is no way she could have not written one; it's her job. But I don't know what she wrote, because I never saw the report.

"When he came back to the classroom, I stood by and supervised the cleanup. After he finished, I wrote an excuse slip and sent him to his next class. Teacher excuse slips are turned into the office, read, and filed. I didn't give him an explanation for his tardiness. The teacher in his next class didn't say anything about not having an explanation or him being covered with blood. No one else in the school said anything.

"I expected to get called down to the office. They must have known. But they never called me down. It was never mentioned to me by anyone, not even in my annual evaluation. As far as the administration and school district were concerned, the incident never occurred.

"But the story was all over town. Everyone knew what happened. The boy's parents didn't complain about his injuries or even paying for his textbooks. His family was in disgrace and totally humiliated. Nowadays, I would have been fired. I guess I was lucky."

Lucky? No, Mr. Woodhead. You were brave.

Chainsaw or Axe?

It is one's willingness to contribute that establishes you in a community. This was a "teaching moment" for the town of Lee, New Hampshire.

Being a city kid, my dad, Harold, had no experience at all with outdoor equipment of any kind. But when they asked for able-bodied volunteers to help clear the lot for the Mast Way Elementary School in Lee, he offered to assist.

"Harold, did you ever use a chainsaw?"

"No."

"Ever drop a tree with an axe?"

"No."

"Not really sure what you can do for us…"

"Are you going to feed the crew?"

"Everybody brings their own food."

"I'll handle it." And he did.

For the entire next week afterwards, we received calls from some Lee housewives, asking to speak to "Mr. Ward." Dad worked 12-hour shifts and wasn't around during the day or early evening to take their calls. Even though some of them sounded desperate, they were too embarrassed to tell Mom what they wanted. But whatever the issue was, it had to be solved. As a last resort, they contacted Marian Stevens, a woman who was known to be a friend of Dad's. She called him at 8:45 one evening.

"Hi Harold, this is Marian Stevens. Some women in town asked me if you could tell them what you put on the hamburgers you cooked at the site clearing last weekend."

"What?"

"Well, some husbands in town won't eat their wife's hamburg or beef until they taste like yours. The women are beside themselves."

Their husbands worked in the woods and fields. As country wives they were responsible for the care and feeding of their family. There was nothing more devastating than having your primary meal rejected by your husband. Dad was, if nothing else, a gentleman, so he told her.

The next Saturday, Dad stopped into the First National Food Store in Newmarket. Charlie Labranche, the store manager, came up to him:

"Harold, what the heck did you do?"

"What are you talking about?"

"All these women are calling the store and coming down from Lee asking for Worcestershire sauce. I usually sell one bottle every six months. Now it's flying off the shelf; I can't keep it in stock. The next order is gone too."

"Salt, pepper and Worcestershire sauce."

Dad laughed so hard he cried.

And so it was that the "Colored man," who didn't know how to use a chainsaw or an axe, introduced Worcestershire sauce to the good people of Lee, New Hampshire.

Son of a SeaCook

Cowardice is fundamental to the racist stereotype ascribed to Black Americans. The Wards of Lee would beg to differ.

A group of young boys were talking about their father's combat experiences in "The Big One."
"My dad was a B17 waist gunner."
"My dad was a tank commander in Europe."
"My dad was a Marine at Tarawa."
"My dad was in the Navy on a heavy cruiser."
"Ward, your father didn't fight. They didn't even let Colored people touch guns in the Navy. He was a friggin' cook..."

Plinking Cans

Except for the soughing of wind in the pines behind me, it was a quiet, sunny spring day on top of the hill. A little bit after noon, the temperature had climbed to 65 degrees.

The chicken barn beside the country road was four stories tall. With binoculars from the cupola of the barn, you could see the Air Force base due east, and Mt. Washington, the state's tallest mountain, due north.

Behind the barn on the south side downslope sat a rusted 55-gallon drum. It was 120 feet from the road and another 20 feet below grade. The prevailing northerly wind deflected off the back of the barn.

The Chicken Barn

Five 16-ounce old Schaeffer beer cans, each one filled with sand. They formed a pyramid of three cans, with a singleton to each side on top of the drum. On the ground by my feet, a single shot bolt action 22 caliber rifle. I had brought a small paper bag. Looking inside, I grimaced, "Remington, cheap ammunition."

Before the box of 50 rimfires was empty, the barrel would be foul, the weapon misfiring. After counting out ten shells into my hand, I dropped the bag on the ground. With my pocket knife I carefully prepped each of them and dropped them in my right pocket.

I looked to my right. I looked to my left. No one was coming up the hill on the road from either direction. Bending down, I picked up the rifle. Safety on. Cycle the bolt. Chamber empty. Shell in the chamber. Bolt closed.

The air was still in the lee of the barn. Behind it though, 100 feet away, the wind glided slowly from right to left at about five miles per hour. Shooting offhand, setting my feet, raising the rifle, through open sights I set the drop. Sighting on the left singleton, I breathed slowly, smoothly, and deeply. Now with the safety off, I exhaled softly and then squeezed slowly.

The can bucked, skipped, and fell. Cycle the bolt. Reset the safety. The left singleton was on its side. Reload, aim, fire, the can jumped off the drum and into the tall grass. I repeated the reloading cycle.

But before firing again, I checked to make sure that a car was not coming while I was in position. If one came, I would set the safety, grab the stock of the rifle with my left hand, and hold it vertically until the vehicle passed.

I was dialed in. By working steadily from left to right, I prevented the wind from drifting a bullet into the wrong target. I aimed and fired until all the cans had been blown off the drum. I walked down the hill, reset the targets and walked back up. I checked for traffic, then repeated the cycle.

I was into my third cycle of cans. A fairly new pickup truck pulled up a hundred feet away and stopped. I paused and looked at the truck. I didn't recognize it. I finished the cycle. All the targets were down.

The truck purred up and stopped. The driver was clean-shaven, with steel-rimmed glasses, dark hair parted on the right, slicked over to the left, and a gray work shirt.

He smiled. "I've been hearing all this shootin' from the other side of the ridge for the past coupla days. Thought I'd come up and check it out. What ya shooting at?"

"Beer cans filled with sand," I replied.

"That's a pretty good distance."

"Only place I can shoot where a ricochet won't hit someone."

"Gotta be safe. That wind's pretty tough. Say, can you hit the rim of the barrel?"

He was a stranger. I thought for a moment why I was here.

"I'll give it a try."

While we spoke, the wind kicked up to about 15 miles per hour. I missed the first shot.

"That's some cross wind."

"Yeah, it just kicked up."

I clenched my teeth, cycled the weapon, fired, and missed again. I hadn't missed in 20 rounds. Now I was missing the damn barrel!

He got out of his truck and stood about ten feet to my right. "You gotta shoot upwind and above your target. Look at the tall grass between you and the barrel. See how far it's bent over? Aim about a foot to the right and about six inches above the barrel." He gestured as he spoke quietly in a matter-of-fact voice.

I ran through my reload sequence, smoothly, with no wasted motion, and applied with his corrections. Just before firing, I instinctively readjusted down several inches and back to the left. I fired. The bullet struck the drum an inch below the rim with a resounding BONG. A silver smear stood out bright against the rust.

Seeing my auto correction, he exhaled with a hiss. "That's good shooting."

"Thanks."

"It's called 'windage.' Say, what are you using for ammunition?"

".22 long rifle hollow points with an 'X' cut in the tips. They split into four pieces when they hit and make a bigger hole when they come out."

This was called a "Dum Dum" bullet, and it was banned by treaty in international warfare. In World War II, a soldier caught with them could be summarily executed.

"Mmmm." He looked away, pausing as if in thought. Then he pursed his lips, nodded his head, and smiled tightly.

"Yes, yes they would. Have a good afternoon." He climbed back into his truck and drove away.

Night Calls

We were the first and only Colored family in town. If one can ever get used to racial harassment, I guess we did. Dad was at sea most of the time as Petty Officer 1st Class in the Navy. One time while he was deployed, we received a phone call telling us to get out of the house in 15 minutes.

"We're coming to burn it down,"

We turned on all of the lights. No one came.

Dad was from New York City when he joined the Navy in 1940. He had graduated from trade school as an electrician's apprentice. He knew nothing about segregation. The Navy made him a Mess Attendant, in essence an officer's servant. He seethed all through World War II at policies demeaning his manhood and intelligence. He was especially incensed by the policy that wouldn't allow him to "fire a shot in anger." The one that prevented him from avenging the death of his best friend, Mess Attendant 1st Class Leonard R. Harmon, who was posthumously awarded the Navy Cross after the Naval Battle of Guadalcanal.

By the end of the war, the Navy was desegregated. But the specialties he was interested in weren't accepting Negroes. He chose to become a Cook, a Commissaryman.

In 1957 aboard DD853, the USS Charles H. Roan, he finally got his opportunity to man a battle station. In the gunnery competition, he outshot everyone on board with the single mount 20 mm Oerlikon. After he retired to New Hampshire, he taught my brother Ted and me how to shoot a .22 caliber rifle for varmint control.

One night, Mom answered the phone.

"Hello. What? Who are you?" She started to cry.

Dad grabbed the phone. "Who is this? Listen, you son of a bitch. You can't talk to my wife that way. I can get this call tracked. When I do, I'm coming after you with my pistol." He slammed down the receiver.

"Why did you say that? You don't have a pistol. You're never here. You're working all the time. If they come after us, we're helpless."

Two Evenings Later

Mom and my two sisters were in the kitchen cleaning up the dinner dishes. Dad called me into the living room. He handed me a brand new single shot bolt action .22 that he'd bought at Johnson's Hardware at the Lee traffic circle.

"You're young, but I don't have a choice here, Michael. Ted's in the Marines. The girls can't do this. I'm working six days a week. If I'm not home, you have to protect your mother and sisters.

"I'll get you at least a box of shells a week for practice. I set up a drum across the street in the field for you to put targets on. I'll show you how to prepare the shells. Stand up on the edge of the road and fire down at it.

"Don't say anything about this to anybody. You understand? If a car comes into the yard at night that you don't recognize, get the Winchester out of the front room closet. It's already loaded with a full clip. There's a box of bullets on the floor. Put a handful in your front pocket."

Then he called Mom and my sisters into the living room. His voice had a hard, sharp edge as he laid out the field of fire.

"Michael, stand here." He positioned me two feet from the living room wall facing the front door eight feet away. I was at an offset two feet to the left of the door centerline. He moved Mom to the door.

"Virginia, when Michael has the rifle up, open the door. Take three steps backwards, holding on to the doorknob with your left hand. After its open, step backwards about 10 feet." Grabbing her by the shoulders, he repositions her.

He took my sisters and placed them by the coffee table at the right-hand edge of the front door. Pointing at the floor, he asserted, "Girls, I want both of you here by the table! I've taped an 'X' on the floor. Do not go past it. Just stand right here. When the man steps into the house, he will look at you first. Do not move until after he looks at you. Do not move!

"This will distract him and give Michael more time to aim. Then turn and walk quickly through the kitchen over to the sewing room. Lie down on the floor by the far wall and stay there. Do not run, stop, look back, or talk to Michael. Your mother will come and take care of you. Do not say anything to Michael. Do you understand?"

"Yes, Dad."

His intensity was riveting. "Michael, if anyone you don't know steps through the doorway into the house, shoot them in the middle of the body. But only after they set foot in the house! Do not shoot them in the head. Shoot them in the body. Do you understand?"

"Yes, Dad."

"Gin, when Michael starts shooting, go stand inside the sewing room door."

He had been transformed. He was a living, shaking thermonuclear rage. Pointing his finger like a knife, stabbing at the place on the floor where they would fall. Screaming.

"Michael, keep shooting them until they stay down. If they get up, shoot them again. If you run out of bullets, reload. I want them down! Down! Right here! DOWN! Do not let them get past you."

Mom and my sisters were screaming and crying. "No, Michael, don't do that!" Mom shouted. "Harold, stop!"

He grabbed my shoulder harder than I've ever had been grabbed before, barking.

"Michael, don't you listen to your mother. Your job is to defend the family; do you understand?"

He was my hero. I would take them down. "Yes Dad."

"Gin, when he signals, get the girls from the sewing room. Take them out to the side porch. You and Michael stand in the kitchen doorway and block the girls' view of the body when you take them out. Do not let the girls see the body! Go to the Haendler's and call the police after you get there. Do not call from the house."

One of my sisters wailed, "Why do we have to leave the house?"

"They may have reinforcements. I don't want you trapped inside the house if they try to burn it down.

"Michael, reload the rifle. You will be the first one out the door. Stand on the side porch and shoot anything moving in the yard. Even if it's a dog, shoot it until it doesn't move. Then, Gin, when Michael says it's clear, get in the car with the girls. Michael, stay on the porch until your mother and sisters are in the car. Then safety the rifle, get in the car, and get out of here."

One Week Later

After work one evening, Dad came home in a good mood. "Did somebody watch you shoot?"

"There was some guy in a pickup truck watching me a while ago. I don't know who it was. Am I in trouble?"

He laughed. "I was at the American Legion having a drink. A guy I didn't know came up to me.

'You live in Calixte's old house, right?'

'Yes. Why?'

"Do you have a young boy doing target practice up there with a .22?"

"Yes."

"That boy can shoot." Then he bought me a beer.

Dad gave me a dollar. "Thanks, Mike."

The word came out of American Legion Post 67 in Newmarket, and it was very clear. "'Young Wahd' up on the Hook Road can shoot like a bastid."

The threatening phone calls stopped.

That spring of 1961, I was nine years old.

American Hero: A Regular Guy

The United States Army Oath of Enlistment reads: "I do solemnly swear that I will support and defend the Constitution of the United States and the State of New Hampshire against all enemies, foreign and domestic."

It was September 1961. The foliage on Bennett Road in Durham, New Hampshire was an autumnal display of natural pyrotechnics. Explosions of brilliant yellow, deep red, luminescent green, and blaze orange painted the trees. Riding through it in the school bus was akin to being inside a rolling kaleidoscope. The bus groaned up over the broken-backed hump of the Boston and Maine Railroad bridge. The kids in the back of the bus catapulted from their seats as the rear wheels crested the rise. They were whooping like banshees as they flew out of their seats.

Mr. Doucette, the driver, was in his mid-forties. Although too young to serve, he, like many of his generation, carried within him memories of incomprehensible events from the war. And just like every man in Lee, he was building a life, one brick at a time for his wife and sons.

He worked two jobs, driving the bus and working as a janitor at Mast Way Elementary School in Lee. Unfailingly polite, he had a quick smile and a "hello" or "hi" for us when we got on the bus and a "goodbye" when we got off. Clean-shaven and wearing steel-rimmed glasses, his hair was held in place with Brylcreem. He was always neatly dressed in gray Dickies work shirt and pants.

He navigated the bus down the hill, around a corner, and stopped at a mailbox. A tall thin wiry man stood next to it at the end of a dirt driveway, leading up to a single-wide trailer. As the bus approached, he was grinning. As it came to a stop, he saw me and my sister. His expression slid to alarm and ran to anger. He froze and glared at us. His boys leapt off the bus and ran to him. He shooed them away.

"Go! Go on up to the house! Driver! What are those niggers doing on the bus?"

"What? What did you say?"

"You heard me! My kids don't ride on a bus with no niggers. Put them off!"

Mr. Doucette put the bus in reverse, shut off the engine, and yanked up on the emergency brake. "You can't talk about kids like that. Where are you from?"

"Oklahoma. It's illegal for niggers to ride on a bus with white kids."

"This is New Hampshire; all kids ride on the bus."

"Not with my kids they don't."

"If I put them off, what are they supposed to do, walk?"

"I don't care what they do, but they can't ride on the bus. If you don't put them off, I'll put them off myself."

The Okie moved towards the door of the bus. Mr. Doucette took off his glasses and put them on the dashboard. He then sprang off his seat and out of the bus. He shoved the larger man backwards. The Okie drilled him in the right eye with a fist. Mr. Doucette countered with a rapid combination, dropping the Okie to his knees.

"You send your wife down to get the kids tomorrow. If she has the same mouth on her as you, your kids won't be allowed to ride my bus."

Mr. Doucette climbed back on the bus, started the engine, released the brakes, put it in first, and we rolled away.

"I'll have your job, you son of a bitch!" the Okie screamed after us.

Mr. Doucette spoke to me as he drove, tears coming from his eyes, either from the punch or the emotion of the moment. I have no idea which. "I was a kid then. We were all kids. We fought those bastards all the way across Europe. Do you know what the hell those Nazis did? Do you know about those camps? Did you read about it in school? No, you're too young."

The memories flooded back, his voice tightening up, like a coil spring wound to its stop and beyond. "I was too young to serve. But my best friends died over there fighting them. We didn't spend four years at war to have to deal with that crap here."

He slammed his fist on the steering wheel. "I'm an American. This is my country. We fought against it over there. Goddammit, I will not stand to see it happen here!"

He paused. "Sorry about the language."

The Okie lodged a complaint with the school board. They dutifully heard him out. Roger Gibb, the bus company owner, told the board, "Nobody has the right to abuse the kids on my buses." The school board agreed. Mr. Doucette kept his job. The Okies moved to a town in the interior of New Hampshire.

Mr. Doucette was a "regular guy" whose youth was consumed by World War II. He never took the U.S. Army's Oath of Enlistment for the war. Yet, 20 years later, a "fellow American" attempted to deny equality to two Colored kids that he barely knew, but whose care was entrusted to him.

Without reservation or fear for his own well-being, he applied the standard: "Against all enemies, foreign and domestic." On that sunny fall afternoon in 1961, the late Mr. Gerard Doucette of Route 152 in Lee, New Hampshire became, in the truest sense of the definition, "an American hero."

Your Best Interests

*Modern-day scam artists invade your life electronically via
the telephone or internet. But in the early sixties it was purely
"old school."*

It was an early May afternoon in 1962. I had just gotten off
the school bus and oddly enough, Dad was at home. He was
sitting on the side porch. He asked me to sit down with him.
He was serious.

"Michael, I've made a mistake. The judge told me that one
condition of my probation was to talk to you. From now on,
if we're threatened, you're to call the police. No guns! No
matter what! Do you understand?"

"Yes Dad."

A Month Before

A realtor had stopped by the house. He was, in his own
estimation, superior in his manner of dress, speech, intellect,
and automobile. His self-image proclaimed; "I am successful
and I am better than you."

Taking a drag off his cigarette, he took a left off Little Hook
Road and rolled up the hill on the Hook Road. He probably
smirked and thought, "These Coloreds aren't very smart. I've
got this one in the bag."

I was standing in the front yard when a brand new 1962 Buick Special V8 pulled into our driveway. It was gloss silver, with a white top, white leather interior, whitewall tires, and chrome wire wheel hubcaps. Music from an AM radio flowed out the open window from a sparkling interior of leather, glass, and chrome. It oozed like fake maple syrup, sugary sweet and without substance, from a warm polished pitcher.

The driver sat calmly smoking a cigarette, waiting to be acknowledged. He was a sharp-featured man; his face was deeply tanned, craggy, and hawk like. He wore a white straw fedora with a black band. His skin tone took me by surprise. It must have shown.

"I just got back last week; I spend my winters in Florida. What's your name?"

"Michael Ward."

He spat on the ground at my feet. Ignoring my name, he said, "Boy, go get your mother. Tell her that Mr. Robert Best is here to see her on a business matter." He accentuated his request with a dismissive plume of smoke. I got angry when he addressed me as "boy", but I did what he asked.

"Mom, there's a man in a car outside who wants to see you. He says it's a business matter. He called me 'boy.'"

Her eyes narrowed.

As we went outside, the man got out of his car, rose, and straightened his hat. His aura of invincibility was secure.

Virginia Ward 1956

My mother was a beautiful woman. On that morning, she had done her hair and put on a yellow frock with a white front to go to the store. He surveyed her with total openness, as if judging a head of livestock. Then he turned on his "smooth winning ways." Hand extended, he introduced himself in a sinuous baritone.

"Good morning Virginia, I'm Robert Best. I live in Durham. I believe my daughter went to high school with your son Ted."

"Yes, what can I do for you?"

"Now, Virginia, I'm a realtor. I just got back from Florida. I heard that you folks were still hanging on up here. Between the two of us, I know that Harold and you spent way too much money on this property. It would be a shame if you folks got in trouble with this place. I mean, God forbid, if Harold loses his job, where would you go? What would you do? You've got no family up here. They're all down in New Jersey, right?"

Mom was calm and composed, revealing nothing. "I see."

"So I decided that I'd come up here today to see if there was something I can do. Now I know Harold; he's a good man. But we both know he's hard-headed and won't listen to reason. So, I thought I'd see if I could help out by offering to take this place off your hands before you lose it." He pulled a legal document from the folio under his arm and extended it to her with a pen.

"I've got some papers here. If you sign them, your family will be protected against Harold's foolhardiness. Virginia, now let's be honest, you folks don't belong up here. This will let you move back down south where you should be, with your own people."

"Well, I appreciate your coming by, but we have things under control."

He paused, surprised at the affront. "You know, a lot of realtors around here aren't like me. They don't even talk to Colored people. They wouldn't be in your dooryard trying to help out. I'm not like that. I know good people when I see them. I just want to see you get out from under before something bad happens."

"Well thank you, I appreciate your offer."

His voice became edgy; his prey was slipping away. "Virginia, this is just between you and me. Harold isn't part of this."

"I'll talk to him about it." Virginia turned and started to walk back to the house.

The suave charm evaporated harshly. He caught Virginia by the arm and spun her around. "Dammit woman, don't you turn your back on me and walk away when I'm talking to you."

She snatched her arm away from him. "Let go of me! Don't you touch me again."

He tried to recover, this time pleading, "Look Virginia, I have your and the children's best interests at heart here. Harold doesn't even have a real job. He's a cook, for Christ's sake. That's no job for a man. He's working 60 hours a week. He'll never pay this place off. I'm trying to help you. We're wasting precious time."

"You can leave now." She turned her back again and walked away.

He shouted at her back. "This is your last chance. If you don't take it, you'll be bankrupted and in the street in a year. Bankrupt!" He swore under his breath, spitting on the ground, and throwing down his cigarette butt without putting it out. He got into his car, slammed the door, started the engine, and dumped it into drive. His tires spat dirt as he sped out of our driveway.

Several weeks later, he ran this con game again, successfully this time, and shattered a family in the Five Corners section of Lee. I remember, because the kids were crying in school. "Mom signed a paper with the realtor when Dad was at work. When Dad got home, he found out about it and beat Mom. Now we have to move in a month."

Some of the "gentlemen" of the surrounding area were not "gentle" men. Dad had let it be known early on that laying a hand on Mom would have serious lasting and negative repercussions. When he came home that night, she told him about the incident. Then he asked me what had happened. His eyes got large, he swore, and he then grabbed his hat and coat. Mom begged him not to do anything. "It's all right; he didn't hurt me."

He ignored her. He ran outside, jumped into our '60 Chevy Biscayne, and flew out of the yard. I don't know where Dad encountered him, but the realtor was "well-schooled" when Dad finished "educating" him.

A man of his station could not be seen to have been bested by a "Colored man." He swore out a complaint for assault, battery, and damages for lost wages.

"Your honor, I am unable to work at my profession showing real estate properties. I have a black eye, split lip, and bruises due to the beating I received from that violent Colored man."

The judge hearing the case was furious at both men. First, the claim for lost wages was thrown out. "The injuries you have suffered are a direct result of an unannounced, uninvited intrusion on this man's property where you tried to swindle his wife. You then attempted to forcibly restrain her by placing your hands on her person. Your claim is denied."

Then Dad took his turn in the tub. "Mr. Ward, I realize that a man has to protect his family. What happened to your wife is not acceptable anywhere. I also understand that you are a veteran and have recently relocated to Lee. You are no longer in Brooklyn, Mr. Ward. New York City justice is not acceptable in New Hampshire. We do not resolve disputes by beating people up in the street. If something like this ever happens again, you will have your wife call the police immediately."

"Yes, Your Honor."

The judge continued. "You have a young son in school with mine, I believe. As part of your probation, you will go home and talk to him. You will explain to him that under no circumstances is he to ever to do what you did. If someone threatens him, his mother, or sisters, he is to call the police."

Dad was fined $50. He was told to stay away from the realtor and placed on probation for six months. If he stayed out of trouble, the charges would be dropped.

But the realtor's partial victory was the beginning of the end of his enterprise. For a couple of years, he had been running this scam quietly on those living on the "financial fringe," the poor and seemingly "uneducated" families of the area. The recipe was simple: "Catch the wife at home alone. Chat her up. Scare the daylights out of her. Have her sign over rights to sell the property. Boot them into the street. Dump the property as quickly as possible."

But now he had been exposed in open court. His ego could not accept that he wasn't still in Florida. Rather than cut his losses, he continued his unseemly work. Shortly afterwards, he ensnared the family of a well-liked hourly employee of the University of New Hampshire. The faculty was made aware of what had happened to us by our neighbor, Dr. Helmut Haendler. The faculty was not happy. They provided the family with a heavy-duty lawyer and sued.

The judge hearing the case was not impressed with his defense of: "I'm just a businessman." The judge then "beat him like a rented mule." The State Board of Realtors temporarily suspended his license and he returned to Florida where, in his own words, "a man could do business."

Later on, one of our neighbors, Harriet Burleigh, remarked to Virginia about the encounter. "I heard that Best came by and you stood him down. He's been successful using that trick on new and poor families in town."

Virginia studied her friend closely for a second and then smiled with amusement. "In New York City, a successful man drives a Lincoln or a Cadillac. He was just a cheap hustler, driving a small Buick."

The Teacher

Achieve and maintain the high ground.

Mildred Haendler was my second mom. She was the mother of my best friend, Steven. They lived four-tenths of a mile down the road. She was a sweet, mild-mannered lady, at least until she got her "Brandon Scottish" up!

This afternoon, she was giving me a ride home from her house, and she was angry. "Michael, that lady is a terrible person. The shame of it is that she's educated, a teacher. She's an embarrassment to her university and her profession. Lord help us if that's what she teaches her students. There was no excuse for her to act like she did, especially after someone went out of their way to help her. I'm really sorry for you, and especially for Virginia. Helmut and I are both furious. I didn't think we had people like that around here. The world doesn't need people like her."

Several Days Before

It was a clear day in late June 1962. A little bit after noon, the sun was high in the sky and scorching the earth. The 90-degree heat boiled off the ground in waves. The traffic on Lee Hook Road was sparse in the early Sixties, with a vehicle passing by about every 20 minutes. If you heard a car or truck, you went to the window to see who it was. So that's what I did. I heard the sound of an engine coming from the Newmarket end of the road. A fairly new car sputtered over the top of the hill. As it passed the house, the engine quit. It coasted to a stop just out of sight beyond the property line. I couldn't see anyone, so I went back to reading my book.

About five minutes later, George the Border Collie announced the arrival of a visitor in the front yard. He trotted down the driveway and greeted the visitor, barking and wagging his tail. The visitor stopped when he approached. I called George. He turned and bounded up to the front door. As I opened it, he entered the house and rambled off to other pursuits; his duty done.

"Hello. Can I help you?" I asked the visitor.

A heavy blond middle-aged woman stood in front of me. Her face was sweating and florid. She was bent over slightly, catching her breath after walking 100 yards in 90-degree heat. Tilting her head, she looked at me, startled, as if I was somehow unexpected.

"I'm afraid of dogs. I was once bitten badly as a child. Thank you for calling him off."

"He's friendly. He doesn't bite."

"I still don't like them. My car broke down. Do you have a telephone?"

"Yes, we do."

She seemed to be relieved, as if she hadn't expected us to have one. "Are your parents home?"

"Yes, my mother's in the kitchen. Please come in."

But she wouldn't. Standing in the doorway, "Can you get her please?"

I thought, "This is strange." I turned and went back to the kitchen.

"Mom, there's a lady at the front door. I asked her to come in, but she said she had to talk to you first."

Mom came to the front door, wiping her hands on her apron. "Hello. Come in out of the heat." She extended her hand, "I'm Virginia Ward."

The woman reluctantly shook my mother's hand. She was still out of breath and spoke in spurts as she introduced herself.

"I'm a teacher in the Hampton schools. I live over on the west side of town. I'm on my way home from a summer school tutoring session. My car broke down. Could I please use your telephone?"

"Sure, but please, come into the kitchen. Sit down and have something cold to drink."

She shuffled into the kitchen behind Mom, exhausted, head bowed. She looked to be on the verge of tears. I didn't know what the problem was, but something was very wrong.

Mom offered her a chair and took a jug from the fridge. "Would you like something to drink? I have some ice water."

The teacher stared at the jug and frowned. "No, I don't want any water. Do you have some iced tea?"

"No, but I can make some."

It wasn't much cooler inside the house than it was outdoors, but Mom was a proper hostess. She boiled some water and made some strong tea. Then she filled two large glasses with ice and added a slice of lemon to each. "Here you are." Mom handed her the glass.

"Thank you." The teacher paused, and in a challenging tone asked. "Do you have any sugar?"

"Yes, here you are. Would you like for me to call someone to fix your car?"

She shoveled several heaping spoonfuls of sugar into her glass and then replied, "Thank you no, that won't be necessary. I'd usually call my husband, he's a machinist. But he won't be out of work until two. I'll call my son instead; he'll know how to fix my car."

As her composure recovered, her attitude blossomed: from defeated to imperious. "What does your husband do for work?"

"He's a cook at Tula's Restaurant in Exeter."

"A cook, I see. I don't eat in Exeter. I only eat in Hampton restaurants, they're better."

I studied her. Her hair was permed in large ringlets. The floral print dress she wore was store bought and expensive. Her dress strained as a sausage casing might to contain the multiple rolls of flesh that circumnavigated her body. I watched as she drank her tea. She stared back at me coldly, unfriendly.

"Michael, don't bother our guest. Go find something to do."

"Yes Mom." I scooted back to the book I was reading.

Finishing her tea, the teacher stood, went to the phone and placed her call. After hanging up, she opened her purse. Now reinvigorated, she was imperial and aggressive.

"What do I owe you for the call?"

"Nothing. It was to Newmarket, and there's no charge for that."

"My son will be here in 45 minutes to an hour. I'll go outside and wait for him in my car."

"You don't have to do that. It's too hot; you should stay in the house. It's not a good idea for a woman to be sitting alone out there."

"Thank you, but no, I'll be fine. I've troubled you people enough. Goodbye." She said this crisply then left as quickly as she could.

Mom stood in the living room doorway. There were tears of anger and embarrassment in her eyes as she watched the teacher waddling rapidly away from our house.

"That fat racist bitch."

Several Minutes Later

"Mercy it's hot," Mildred Haendler thought as she drove her gray Volvo station wagon up the hill to our house. Lee Hook Road was a dusty state-maintained "improved dirt road." There had been no recent traffic, so she was able to ride with the windows down. She pulled into the side yard, got out of the car, and went up to the side porch door.

"Oh Virginia, I came as soon as I could after your phone call. Is that horrible woman still out there?"

"I think so. You can't see her car from here. It's in front of Mr. Earl's. I only called because she wouldn't stay in the house. I don't like her, but it's not safe for a single woman to be stranded alone out here."

"It's all right. I'll stay with her until someone arrives."

"I have some ice water. But I don't think she'll drink it because she'll recognize the jug."

The look passing between Mom and Mildred encapsulated both anger and pity.

"It's OK, I brought some cold water in a thermos."

Mom nodded and held tight to her jug.

Déjà vu: Mississippi Burning

Assessing the state of civil rights in America will always be a fraught endeavor. Personal experiences indelibly stamp an individual's accounting. Sometimes, as in my case, the effect did not manifest itself for many years.

It was a late afternoon in August 1964. My family sat in the living room watching television, transfixed.

Dad sat hunched over, stone silent, his face drawn tight, elbows on knees, his gaze fixated on the television. His eyes reflected horrors that had escaped from the vault in his memory that protected him from the past. He held a glass of whiskey with both hands. It trembled every now and again. A thousand-yard stare boring into the screen. A PTSD moment, he was living in his own private hell, a reflection of his youth, the U.S. Navy, or New Hampshire. Who could tell?

Mom sat upright on a kitchen chair. Her arms were outstretched, her hands locked, squeezing her knees; frozen; rigid. Large tears, like rivers from her soul, rolled down her face. One of my sisters cried loudly. The other was too shocked to speak. Taking Dad's cues, I sat in silence.

James Chaney, Andrew Goodman, and Michael Schwerner were three Civil Rights workers who had gone missing in Mississippi for over a month. Foul play was suspected. The FBI had launched a massive task force to find them.

We watched in agony as three bundles swathed in black plastic were excavated from an inhuman place in Philadelphia, Mississippi. At one point, all of the activity took place out of camera range. For 15 to 20 minutes, the only image on TV was that of a white Cadillac ambulance. It sat silently, its rear door with a big painted cross, ajar. A mouth agape, waiting to receive its cargo: three young men.

One of my sisters sobbed, "Dad, nothing's happening. I don't want to watch this. Can I please go?"

"Shhhh, stay! We all have to see this."

Other than sheer hatred, there was no logical explanation for what we were watching. Fourteen hundred miles away in Lee, New Hampshire, we too were similarly entombed, living in an uncertain world filled with indeterminate enemies.

Questioning: "Are we next?"

In August 2017, a young lady, Ms. Heather Heyer, was killed protesting an Alt Right rally in Charlottesville, Virginia. Accounts of her death rekindled my memories of 53 years prior.

It was my own PTSD moment, my own private hell. Memories of an early childhood spent in fear of a strange car arriving in the driveway at night. It blew through my mind and body like a gasoline bomb. My family was totally unaware of my distress. Given my upbringing, I didn't share it with them.

My skin iced; my stomach knotted and roiled. I was numbed and immobilized for almost 12 hours.

Questioning: "Are we next?"

May you never have to ask yourself that question. If so, you'll be living it. Then you must come to terms with it, before you explain it to your children. I wouldn't wish that on anyone.

Has the clock of civil rights in America been reset to the summer of 1964?

The Stump

Pets in the Ward household were dual-purpose entities. To be cute or funny was insufficient; they were expected to contribute. If they met the criteria, they were anthropomorphized as part of the family. If not? Well, their mileage might vary.

A pair of good-sized wood splitting stumps were stacked one on top of the other in the front yard. The top stump was a little smaller than the bottom one. But if it was taken down it was too heavy for me to lift back up. All I could do was roll it into position for Dad to put back when he got home.

One fall afternoon in 1963, I got off the school bus and did what country kids did: I cruised around the yard looking for evidence of animals, feathers, bones, or snakes, and so on. Finding none, I noticed that the top stump had been moved about 20 feet from its mate. It had a big dark brown stain on it. I thought it odd because it hadn't rained that day.

In the morning, the Ward family left the house and headed off to work or school. During the day, our pets lived outside and went wherever it is that country pets go. In the afternoon, they would show up to meet the school bus, hang out until dinner, and then spend the night in the house.

Gorgeous George was a border collie; beautiful, gregarious, playful, and charming. He masterfully eliminated the woodchuck population with skill and aplomb. For him it was great fun. Once a year, he would perform a demonstration for us. Herd the chuck onto the front lawn. Run circles around it until it was tired. Then suddenly reverse direction. Charge in, grab it by the nape of the neck, and sit back on his haunches. Then torquing his body in the opposite direction that the chuck had been moving, give it a hard shake, and snap its neck. Then he would drag it out of sight and chow down.

Gorgeous George

He was a welcome sight in most of our neighbors' yards. The women liked him because they didn't have to shoot and dispose of woodchucks. The other method--shoot it and then wait for Dad to get home to deal with it--could be problematic.

A typical "pre-George" evening scenario at one of our neighbor's houses went something like this.

"Honey! I'm home!"

"Have a seat." She hands him a beer.

"Say when you're finished, will you do me a favor?"

"Sure."

"I shot a woodchuck in the side yard this morning. I don't want the cat playing with the body. Would you bury it? And please don't forget this time."

On a previous occasion, the neighbor had forgotten to bury one. It had been a Friday; they went to visit relatives over the weekend. The temperature was in the high 80's lower 90's. When the woodchuck's corpse exploded on Monday afternoon, it was obvious that "something was rotten in Lee" - not just in Denmark.

"Okay." He winced at the memory.

Consequently, George was welcomed by both Ma and Pa in that particular household.

So efficient was he that some of our neighbors began to compensate him outrageously for his expertise. In one case in particular, Mom got pissed.

"Harold, George is eating better than us. They're feeding him sirloin hamburger; we're eating ground chuck."

He howled with laughter: "Maybe you should take the kids and go with him!"

When it was hot out, however, George tended to exhibit a rather noxious trait. He loved rolling in the cow manure slurry pond at the farm at the foot of the hill. He could not understand why he wasn't universally loved after these immersions, but otherwise he was a great dog.

Boats was a handsome, tiger-striped tomcat with a white bib and feet. He was a grandson of Scrappy, the alley cat that we had brought with us from Brooklyn. Scrappy had been 13 pounds of horny urban mean. He had driven away all of the black and white tomcats from the farm down the hill. His tiger-striped gene pool reigned supreme for almost 20 years.

During Boat's tenure, our home had no mouse, large insect, or other small rodent incursions. He was also a rascal. If he caught George sleeping, he would slink over and give him a swat across the face. George would wake up with a start and take off after him. Boats would dive under the TV stand where George couldn't fit. George would stand there barking furiously at him until someone managed to calm him down. In reality, they were good friends.

The third miscreant was a totally nontraditional pet. Mabel was a white hen. She wasn't really friendly. You would only get away with petting her once, and then she would peck you, hard.

One afternoon, shortly after Mabel joined the family, the school bus driver stopped to let us off. He opened the door and saw a border collie, a tiger-striped cat, and a white chicken all charging up to the bus. He sat hunched over the steering wheel, laughing for several minutes before he drove off.

When it came to sleeping in the house, she was the exception. You cannot housebreak a chicken. We tried. We failed. Virginia did not tolerate stupidity in humans or animals. She especially did not tolerate animals that refused to master bowel or bladder control inside her house. "I raised four kids. I'm not cleaning up after an animal that's too stupid to ask to go outside."

With that, Mabel was banished to the outdoors. From her perspective, she was quite happy to cruise around the yard and do "chicken things" such as eating bugs. But with Mom's animus towards "non-contributing pets" and unseemly behavior, unbeknownst to her, Mabel was in limbo.

It was fall and getting cold. Dad had just changed jobs. Money was tight during that "in-between period." One evening, we came home to the aroma of an astonishing dinner. Mom's preparation had been exquisite, sautéed mushrooms and onions basted in wine, baked potatoes with sour cream, and snap peas. We were tucking right into it when one of my sisters froze.

She said, "Mom! Where's Mabel?"

Mom uttered a nervous laugh and said, "Oh, I don't know, outside somewhere."

My sister continued, "She didn't meet the bus. She must be hurt or something. I'd better go find her."

Dad said, "I didn't see her when I got home either."

My sisters and I started to get up from the table.

"Stop. All right, all right! I cooked her."

Everyone dropped their forks and looked at their plates.

"For Chrissakes, Virginia..."

"Noooo Mom! That was Mabel's blood on the stump!"

My sister shrieked, "We can't eat this. We are not cannibals…"

Apparently, neither were George nor Boats. Mom tried to serve Mabel to them, but they wouldn't eat her either. George sniffed the bowl, gave her a disgusted look, turned his back, and walked away. Boats thought he was next and disappeared under the couch.

An Artifact

In New Hampshire, in the fifties through seventies, there was an unstated reality among the "Colored kids." We did not go out on dates or to the junior prom with our schoolmates. However, some context must be provided. The Civil Rights Act had only been in effect for three years in 1967 when I began my freshman year at Oyster River High School in Durham. At the same time, interracial marriage was still illegal in many southern states. But even liberal Durham was not immune to the prevailing thought that Colored people were merely "curiosities."

For family, pets, and home, love is imbued at an early age. Then later in life, at junior high dances, when cute bumbling children enter their first relationship rocket rides. Emotions never experienced before explode into life, like corn stalks popping, growing in the midsummer heat. Young people discovering their place in life as couples.

I was part of that ride until late in the 7th grade. Then, girls who had always danced with me, stopped cold. At first, it was as if I was an afterthought; then, it was overt exclusion.

Three years later, I was the only black male student in a high school of 400. My sophomore year, I asked six different girls I liked who didn't have boyfriends to go to the junior prom. I was turned down by all of them. "No." Or worse: "I don't like you that way."

I was an actor in high school, a radio DJ, and a lead singer in a working "frat" band at UNH. But with each attempt at connecting with girls in my school, I failed. In too many cases, I was teased before being crushed. I hadn't changed. I couldn't figure out what had happened between the first and second halves of 7th grade. But something had. I had known most of the girls in my class since kindergarten. It never occurred to me that it was due to my race.

During the second semester of my junior year, I came to a decision. I refused to be humiliated again. I didn't ask anyone to the prom. And I refused to go stag. Nor would I become a second-class citizen, by "trucking in" a date from another school like my brother and sister had done. "To hell with them."

Instead, I took the role of "The Negro" in "The Roar of the Greasepaint and the Smell of the Crowd" at the Theatre by the Sea in Portsmouth. I was now a 15-year-old professional actor with a solo.

Sitting in the kitchen that early spring afternoon, Mom asked if I was going to the prom.

"No, Mom, I'm not." I then told her about my sophomore year experience.

She exploded, "Those bitches! Neither of my beautiful boys is good enough for them? We came from nothing. We have a successful business. We've done everything you're supposed to do. God! I wish we'd never left Brooklyn."

She got up, went into the sewing room, slammed the door, sat at her sewing machine, and cried. I never spoke to my mother about my relationships again. From then on, I partied at UNH with my band or college students. Did I get lucky? No, but I got loaded, and that was good enough.

Very briefly during my senior year at Oyster River, I tried going to dances again. But this time the rejection took on a more sinister turn.

A female classmate warned me, "Stay away from my little sister, the freshman."

"What?"

"I'm warning you. Stay away from her. Stop dancing with her, and don't even talk to her. If you don't, my father will put your father out of business. She'll get in trouble too."

"What? My dad's in Exeter. He can't touch him."

"Yes, he can. When we were in Dover, there was a businessman who crossed him. Dad absolutely destroyed him. Look, you're a nice guy, but you have to leave my little sister alone."

The Next Night

Just after dinner, Dad got right to the point. "Michael, I spoke to your classmate's father this afternoon."

It had been warm, bright, and sunny that fall afternoon in 1969. Dad closed his restaurant in Exeter early at four. He had driven the 1960 Falcon wagon briskly over to Durham. He had stopped in at a business and inquired of the clerk, "What's my balance?"

As he wrote out the check, he explained, "I'm closing my account. Is the owner in?"

"No, he's gone home for the day."

"I'd like to settle up in person. Where does he live?"

The clerk provided him with the address and directions. He thanked her politely and left.

When he arrived at the business owner's home, he got out of the Falcon. Straightening up, he rolled his shoulders, loosening them as he walked to the front door of the house. He rang the bell.

The business owner opened the door. As king of his domain, he glared at the invader with contempt.

"What are you doing here?"

"Don't threaten my son about dating your daughter and don't fuck with my business."

He snorted, "You don't scare me. I know what you did to my friend, Best. You won't get away with that here. I have friends in the police. If you step out of line, I'll call them. They'll be here in an instant and take care of you like that." He snapped his fingers for emphasis.

Dad growled, "You won't make it to the phone."

The color drained from the man's face with the memory of the absolute beat down Harold had laid on his friend.

Dad threw the check on the floor. "There's your money. Our business is done. Don't fuck with me or my son again." He turned on his heel and left.

With that, I kissed high school dances goodbye forever. I was either "a bug in a jar" or "a trophy in a gilded cage,"… whatever. Like my brother Ted ten years before, I was an artifact, meant to be observed, but not accepted.

Life's Ultimate Joy

I entered college in the middle of the sexual revolution with the emotional maturity of an eighth grader. It didn't go well. My lack of experience was such that I neither knew nor comprehended the language of love. The quick smile and nod, a foot on top of yours under a table, or the breast in your back were all incomprehensible signals.

In high school, I had armored up with alcohol to insulate myself from the inevitable rejection of attempts at relationships. But all it did was "kick the can down the road." For a brief period, when I was 19 and not in college, I drank a fifth a day. I had become inured to the belief that there was "no one for me." I was resigned to being solitary for the rest of my life.

Then, in the summer of 1973, I met the most beautiful girl I'd ever seen. For her, it was love at first sight. As for me, my past led me to believe that I'd just be toyed with and abandoned. I could not allow myself to think that someone so arrestingly beautiful truly wanted me. I was 21, and she tried with everything she knew to pull me from junior high to adult social maturity in a month.

For the first time in my life, I was in love. When she was near me, I became dizzy and my hands shook. My pulse pounded, a sheen of sweat glistened on my forehead. Whether we were together or apart, I could no longer concentrate. I didn't know what was wrong with me. I thought that I had gone mad. I didn't dare tell her how I felt. I was terrified that she'd reject me as being crazy.

The suppression of extreme emotion had been burned into my psyche at age nine. The valve gating the remainder had been bolted down and welded shut in high school. The family credo, "Do not expose your feelings to others," prevented me from seeking counseling. The battle between love and the emotionless "index of integration" was fought to a draw. I lost.

It was the biggest disaster in my life. We were crazy in love. She told me, "You are the most beautiful man I have ever seen." In my entire life, no one had ever said that to me.

She came from a well-to-do family. "Move in with me. All you'll have to do is focus on your career. You won't have to work at the gas station anymore. I'll pay for everything." Then she looked into my eyes and told me, "Michael, you're the one."

I had no idea what she was talking about until a friend explained it to me. But I was unable to release the lock on my soul. I walked away from the first woman who ever said "I love you" to me and meant it. Her roommate told me that, brokenhearted, she cried for a week. I felt sad, but my armor was such that she just faded away.

The accrued cost of being the "index of integration" was the denial of life's ultimate joy.

Janetos Market on the Upper Square

You never know who you're going to meet on the way to work.

It was September 1973. I was broke and working two jobs while going to the University of New Hampshire in Durham. I had just moved out of my parents' house and into an apartment on Portland Avenue in Dover. I couldn't afford a car and hitchhiked or walked everywhere I went. My Mom told me to shop at Janetos Market. "It's a good market. Mr. Bandouverus is a nice man."

One day, needing groceries, I walked the quarter mile from my apartment to Janetos on Dover's Upper Square. I rolled my cart up to the meat counter. The cart was loaded up with typical college student food. I ran the totals in my head. I hate math, and I suck at it. I hate coming up short at the register even more.

"Let's see: a loaf of bread, Kraft mac & cheese, canned tuna with oil, B&M baked beans, a bag of potatoes, an onion, and a canned ham. Ugh! I couldn't get that damn song out of my head. "Why would a Jewish guy, Norman Greenbaum, sing about buying a canned ham?'"

I did a paranoid double check of the cart. Whew, I should have enough to buy a chuck steak for dinner.

From behind the counter, Mr. Bandouverus asked, "Can I help you?" He was a husky Greek man in his forties, with a thick shock of gray streaked dark brown hair.

"I'd like a two-pound chuck steak."

"Okay." Effortlessly pulling the roast from the case, he tossed it on the butcher block. He carved several dinners with a smooth, steady stroke.

"Are you from the university?"

"Yes, but I grew up in Lee. My mom told me to come here."

He tilted his head, wrinkled his brow and looked at me. "Are you related to Virginia Ward?"

"Yes, she's my mother, I'm her son Mike."

Smiling warmly, he said, "Ummm, Virginia. I like her. She is a very nice lady. Do you work?" He studied me.

"Yes, I work at Cobb's Citgo in Durham and the UNH Library."

He nodded his approval. "Good." Then he paused for a moment and came to a decision. "Is this the day that you usually shop?"

"Yes, usually early in the week."

"When you finish shopping and you're ready to pay, you come to the back counter. Ask for me, no one else. I'll check out your groceries. And please give Virginia my regards."

On Tuesday or Wednesday afternoons until I graduated, I shopped at Janetos. He always marked down the meat. "I'm charging you the same as what I pay for my family." Then he put extra, usually veal or chicken in my cart for free.

Forty Plus Years Later

It was 6:50 AM, and the Amtrak Downeaster train 680 was southbound to Boston from Portland, Maine. I had just boarded in Exeter for my daily commute. I took a seat next to a tall blonde woman whom I'd never met before. We engaged in the usual perfunctory and bland introductory commuter "I'm not an interstate psycho killer" type dialogue.

She said, "My name is Jamie. I'm from Dover."

"I'm Mike. I grew up in Lee. I lived in Dover from '73 to '76 when I went to the 'U.'"

"Did you ever shop at Janetos Market?"

"Yes -- every week."

"That was my grandfather."

A surge of warmth flooded through me at the memory of a nice man. I told her a story that had never been heard outside of my family. Just as I finished, the train rolled under the Route 121 Plaistow railroad bridge. Then emerging from the forest, we crossed the border into Massachusetts.

The morning sun rays burst through the window, backlighting, enveloping, and haloing her face. Strands of blonde hair became translucent. Her irises were gray, bright, dilated, and glistening. An open, honest smile blossomed with the joy of an unexpected revelation. Her laugh was bell-like, resonant, and heartfelt.

"That sounds just like him..."

My body chilled, resonating in the transcendent aura of her grandfather's sun-driven spirit.

We were both silent for a moment, lost in our reflections of a generous man.

I blinked and looked into her eyes, "Thank you for your family."

Then I kissed her on the cheek.

Water Rights

It was a fifth magnitude spring created by fractures in the New Hampshire granite bedrock. The hydrostatic pressure of its source aquifer sought out and found minute pathways for the water to escape from its subterranean domain. Over time, they coalesced into a single conduit, which was forcing its way upwards into the light. Water surging, 20 gallons per minute, clear, clean, and cold. A deeded covenant from when the property was subdivided long ago provided the abutting owner with water rights.

In 1974, New Hampshire was not as "liberal" as one might think...

Two men drove down a narrow winding dirt track through the scrub pine woods in the town of Lee on a sunny April morning. They passed a small sand pit. One of the men remarked, "I remember rolling in the grass over there with Betsy after a six pack on a coupla Friday nights."

"Just a couple?" his friend asked. "I heard you came out on Thursday and put up a sign that said 'Reserved.' Everybody used this spot."

Turning right at the end of the track, pulling ahead all the way to the end, they came to a stop. With the engine off, the silence was profound. The wild animal and bird population was quiet, as if holding its collective breath. The first man took a last drag from his cigarette. Then he snuffed it out on the ground. "Don't want to set the woods on fire." They both laughed.

They removed a toolbox, chainfall, a cable, and a piece of 4x4 from the trunk. They carried the equipment over to a small asphalt shingled building.

"Did you measure the width like you said you would?"

"Yeah, four feet should do it."

"Drop the power; I don't want to get cooked."

"Done. Pop that door open, and let's get moving."

"No hurry. They won't need it until 5:30 or so."

Once inside the building, one man remarked, "Gee, it was nice of them to put lights in here."

They hung the 4x4, then mounted the chainfall, and tested it to make sure it didn't slip. "Don't want that thing falling."

"You've got the height, so you go in the hole. I'll even hold on to your feet."

"Generous... I get to do all the work."

He slid down into the opening. "There, the inlet and outlets are closed. Give me the sling." Grunting, he wound it around the motor.

"Grab this end and hang it on the hook. Then gimme a 3/4" socket on an extension."

Several minutes passed. "Done."

He shimmied backwards out of the hole. "OK muscles, haul away!"

Several Hours Later

Mom came home from work at the Lee Town Office where she was the Assistant Town Clerk and Tax Collector. She started preparing dinner around 5:30. She hummed as she moved about the kitchen. Chicken, beans, and "swamp seed," Dad's pet name for rice. She turned to the sink to rinse the beans.

"Dammit! Harold, we don't have any water."

"Hold on Gin. Something must have tripped the breaker. I'll go down and check it out."

Finishing his beer, he got into his truck and drove down to the pump house. It was still light, but he carried a flashlight, in case the bulb had blown out.

The pump house door was ajar, the lock sheared off. A small tendril of smoke, accompanied by the acrid smell of an electrical fire, crept out of the shattered door. Inside, 120 pounds of brand-new pump and impeller had been unbolted, raised, and dropped back into the well sump. The "coup de grace" was applied when the 30A of 220-volt, 3 phase power had been restored to the unit with no load. A four-month-old pumping system had been reduced to a smoking chunk of scrap steel, aluminum and copper.

Dad drove back to the house, furious, and called the police. "Chief, I've told you about this before. They've been messing with my water for years. They used to just pull the breaker. Then they smashed the meter. The last time they ripped out all of the wiring and knocked down the pump house. We just paid $1500 to have an entire new pump installed. Now it's completely destroyed. I'm not worried about the cost; our insurance will replace the pump."

He threw it down. "Since you can't protect my property, I'm going to build a sniper hide in the trees. I'll call Michael back from UNH. Michael, Virginia, or I will be in it 24 hours a day. If anyone comes within fifty feet of our pump house, we will shoot them, no questions asked. Virginia may not hit anything with the Savage 300, but she'll shoot until she runs out of bullets. Michael and I can shoot."

For the second time in our twelve years in New Hampshire, Harold Ward had declared war. It was known in town that we shot well. Dad had briefly been an anti-aircraft gunner in the Navy. Ted was a U.S. Marine. My own skill had been recognized at age nine by a member of Newmarket's American Legion Post #67.

Did you really want to have a gunfight with the Colored man on the hill over his deeded rights to spring water? If so, Harold was ready: locked, loaded, and pissed.

Cellphones didn't exist back then. If you were shot, you'd have to belly crawl an eighth of a mile to Dave and Shirley Clark's house to use the nearest phone. Then a half hour later, Roy Kent would arrive from Newmarket with the ambulance. It would be another 20 minutes to Exeter Hospital. We would not be providing first aid or summoning Roy. If shot, you would die.

The Next Saturday Night

Harold called me home from the "U" to discuss his plan. "They've been trying to run us off this hill for years. If we can't secure our water, we'll have to move. Everyone in town knows that I'm working off my bankruptcy. They think they can drive me off because I'm down. This is their last chance. Do you remember why I taught you to shoot? This is the same thing. They're gonna find out that I'm done being fucked with."

"Dad, you can't do this. The pump house isn't on our property. If we hurt or kill someone, we'll end up in jail!"

"I don't care. If they want this hill, they can pay for it in blood."

Terrified, I invoked the "worst case scenario." "If Mom shoots and kills someone, she's going to be arrested and indicted for first-degree murder."

"No. They won't arrest her."

"They'll have a warrant."

"I don't care. I won't let them take her out of the house."

"Dad, they have guns."

"So do I."

"If you have a gunfight with the police, I'm going to end up with two dead parents. If you kill one, you'll get life."

"Michael, I don't care; they will not enter this house. I will die before I let them take Virginia."

There would be no reasoning with him; his combat rage was fully engaged. I gritted my teeth to keep from puking. This was way beyond shooting an uninvited stranger breaching our house when I was a nine-year-old. This was premeditated murder in the first degree, by, in my case, someone who was no longer a juvenile. If Dad's threat was ignored, one or more of us was going to end up in state prison or dead.

Dad's declaration placed the police chief and the force in an untenable position. They had to stop this before the new pump was installed. If not:

"Virginia Ward, I hereby place you under arrest for aggravated murder in the first degree."

The officer uttering that statement would set into motion a chain of events that could have no conceivable positive outcome. If Harold was home, it would be a bloodbath. Local, state police, and county sheriffs would be required to serve the warrant. The subsequent state police and FBI investigations would focus first on the actions of the Police Department. Then the instigators would be hunted down and federally prosecuted.

But what of Virginia, the nice lady who for 20 years had grown African violets for the plant booth at the town fair? The Assistant Town Clerk and Tax Collector who had been given a raise by a voter motion at the town meeting the year before? If she was arrested, the townspeople would be merciless. The Police Department would be replaced "en masse." And if she were killed, her death would rip the heart from the town of Lee.

No one would emerge unscathed.

The chief was a young man. He had badly underestimated both the severity of the situation as well as Harold's resolve. He and the department had their backs to the wall and knew it.

"Jesus Christ! No Harold! Please, you don't want to do this. I can take care of it."

"You'd better."

We have no idea who the police chief passed the word on to, but the vandalism ceased. After that, Mom and Dad enjoyed an uninterrupted flow of spring water for the next 15 years. Then one day an unfortunate squirrel decided to use the insulation from the input feed for part of his nest. He was subsequently barbequed and instantaneously transformed into a secondary load resistor that burned out the pump. But by that time, they were old enough to not want to deal with a water source a third of a mile away down a dirt road. They dug a well.

Community

Definition of community:
1. A group of people living in the same place or having a
particular characteristic in common.
2. A feeling of fellowship with others, as a result of sharing
common attitudes, interests, and goals.

How does one become a member of a New Hampshire
community? If you can demonstrate self-reliance, honesty,
consistency, generosity, and understand that we are all
different, yet the same, for at least two decades, you are
accepted. We moved from Brooklyn, New York to Lee, New
Hampshire in 1957. After his retirement from the Navy, Dad
was a cook in various restaurants, including his own, and the
Exeter Hospital.

Dad was orphaned at ten at the onset of the Depression. He
was kicked around from one relative to another for most of
his childhood. He had an "upfront and personal" relationship
with hunger and neglect. Mom was the only child of a single
mother. Her upbringing was also rather "spare." With four
kids of their own, they shared a common trait: an
unconditional love of children. In what little spare time he
had, Dad would babysit neighbors' infants when the moms
needed a break. Children loved him. In modern terms, he was
a "kid magnet."

In small New Hampshire towns from the 1950s through the 1980s, if a citizen fell on hard times and was willing to work, work was found. Dad was bankrupt after his second restaurant failed. A position opened up as the janitor of Mast Way Elementary School in Lee. When he took the job at the school, he already knew some of the children from babysitting. They, in turn, told the other kids: "Mr. Ward is nice."

So why was this important? What does a "nice janitor" have to do with elementary school students? If they misbehaved, many teachers would send them to go see Mr. Ward, instead of the principal's office. Dad would put them to work helping him around the school.

During that time, he'd ask them: "What did you do? What would your parents think about it?" He would listen. Then he'd talk them through the situation. He was usually able to get the kids to see the other side of the story.

Ten years later, he was semi-retired. One night, the Lee police chief stopped in for a visit and came right to the point. "Harold, I'd like for you to become a policeman."

"What?"

"We talked it over at the station. We're having a devil of a time with these kids. We can't get through to them. You're the only adult in town whom they respect and will listen to."

So, Dad took the New Hampshire police exam and scored a 93. He then was duly sworn in to ride herd over a group of kids, some of whom he changed as infants and monitored in school detention. When he stopped them, they received the same speech he gave them at Mast Way. "What are you doing? How do you explain this to your parents?"

When he finally retired, he received a commendation for 20 years of distinguished service. He was the only adult that an entire generation of kids respected. He was also the only black man in an all-white town.

Harold and his "other kids" - even their mother!

Cold Feet

"A Buick Electra! Who'd have thought I'd end up driving a Buick Electra police cruiser? Hell, who'd have thought I'd be a cop! Aunt Carrie must be rolling in her casket." -- *Harold Ward*

In New Hampshire, five degrees is cold; 20 is an irritation. A 20-mile-per-hour winter wind slashes at your face like a hot box cutter and raises a subliminal anger in your psyche. Eventually, your face and psyche concede defeat and accept the punishment.

In the days before the days of "warm when wet" polypropylene garments, the epitome of winter misery was being wet. While the factors of wind and cold can be countered, "winter wet" cannot. With this scenario, the misery taxonomy of body parts establishes wet feet at the top of the hierarchy. Nothing is worse. Once wet and cold, they become numb. The loss of feeling portends the crushing electric throbbing pain that inevitably results when full circulation slowly returns and nerve endings reawaken with explosive assent.

It was 14 degrees one night, a third of the way between cold and irritation. The wind speed had the same numeric intensity. The saving grace was that it was dry. Harold sat in a police cruiser next to the town hall in Lee that winter evening. An occasional vehicle rippled past, its engine grumbling, condensation swirling sluggishly from the exhaust.

The driver's side cruiser window was cracked open just enough to provide an air exchange. If not, one would get woozy due to a lack of oxygen, 'cause the damn car sealed up tighter than a drum. You wouldn't want it to get too warm either, because that would make you sleepy and your feet would sweat.

"Patrol, we have a motorist requesting assistance on 155 past 155A."

"Roger that dispatch... On my way."

He pulled up behind the motorist, getting out, adjusting his "mountie" hat. "Sir, did you request assistance?"

"Yes, officer. I struck a deer, and I'd like to recover it."

The doe had not died after being struck. She had dragged herself down the embankment across a swamp and into the woods. They tracked it, occasionally breaking through the swamp ice. When they did, the water flooded over the top of their shoes. They continued for a half mile before they found her.

She lay panting, wounded and exhausted. She possessed the innate certainty of wild things that her ultimate destruction was nigh. How or what; coyote, fishercat, dog, temperature, or man was immaterial. Only the duration and physicality of her extinction was in doubt. On this night, the enemy was man, and the end was mercifully quick.

"Poor thing." Dad pulled out his revolver and dispatched her with a single round. "Let's each grab a leg and get out of here…"

It took a while to drag the doe back across the swamp. This time, every step broke through the ice, bathing their feet in ice water four inches above the ankle. Slowly, inexorably Harold began to lose the feeling in his feet. They stopped every now and again to take a breather. By necessity, the breaks were short, as each one increased the thaw out time and the pain that inevitably accompanied it. By the time they reached the foot of the embankment Dad had no feeling in his feet. They paused before the final drag up to the road, each sucking frigid draughts of air.

"Okay, one last drag."

Then a quick swing of the doe, up, over and into the motorist's trunk. "Thanks."

"No problem."

The motorist got into his car and drove away.

"Dispatch, I need to return to the station. My feet are frozen."

"Roger, patrol."

Harold groused. "Cheap bastard didn't offer me anything: a flank, a roast, not even a steak…"

Country Bliss

When some people move into a new neighborhood, they expect to bring their old one with them.

With cash in hand, he had emigrated from the suburbs of the expansive New York City Metro area to southern New Hampshire. Once a senior executive, he was an individual accustomed to bending others as desired to fulfill his needs. He smirked at the cost differential between his former home and this gorgeous new one. Now that he and his wife were firmly ensconced, they proclaimed themselves to all who would listen as "country folk."

The soothing ambiance of pine-scented air, blending with a lack of artificial noise, created a solitude, a personal state of nirvana. Like all things of his world, this too was a commodity. And as with all commoditized items, ownership conveyed absolute control.

Unbeknownst to this erstwhile "king of all he surveilled" was a confluence of rural realities against which he was defenseless.

The first, second, and third laws of real estate are "location, location, location." They are akin to the laws of thermodynamics in their absolutism, and they cannot be denied.

Should you fail to survey your new environment before assuming ownership, you will endure the consequences. Nature is not cognizant of wealth. Nor do sound waves "give a tinker's damn" about your household income. These are critical factors to be considered prior to relocating to the countryside. When citizens are assaulted in their homes by forces beyond their control, to whom do they turn?

"911. What is your emergency?"

"I need a patrolman at my house immediately."

"What is your emergency?"

"My goddamn neighbor's generator."

"We'll have a patrolman their shortly."

"He'd better be!"

Harold arrives. "Sir."

"The goddamn generator at the farm next door is running all times of the day and night. How am I supposed to live with that? I've tried talking to him, but he keeps blathering about his livestock needing water. Well, I need to sleep at night."

"I'll go speak with him about it."

"Lot of good that will do. I've talked to him, and he still runs the damn thing all hours of the day and night. I ought to just sue him for being a public nuisance."

Dad got into the cruiser and drove over to the farm. The farmer explained that the generator powered a water pump to provide for 80 head of cattle. When the water troughs dropped below a certain level, the limit switches tripped. This started the generator, which drove the pump to refill the troughs. The duty cycle was only about 10 minutes, but it was sporadic. An unmuffled single cylinder diesel firing up at 2:00 AM can indeed disrupt a sleep cycle.

When the generator was installed, the exhaust pointed at a woodlot. When the new house was sited there, it never occurred to the farmer that the noise would be a problem. After a discussion with the police, he rotated the generator exhaust pipe by 180 degrees. Then he built a small shed and insulated it with fiberglass to further reduce the noise. The complaints ceased. This is called "Community Policing."

Several Months Later

"911. What is your emergency?"

"I need a patrolman at my house immediately."

"What is your emergency?"

"My goddamn neighbor's cows…"

"We'll have a patrolman there shortly."

"He'd better be!"

Dad arrived in the cruiser at same address. "Sir."

"Can you hear that noise? How am I supposed to sleep through that racket?"

A group of heifers in labor were proclaiming their predicament to the world in loud and absolute terms.

"I moved out to the country for peace and quiet, not for this. Tell him to make them stop."

"Sir, I don't think he can do anything about it. The heifers are in labor; it's natural."

"I don't care if it's natural. If he can't shut them up, you're going to have to!"

"How in the world am I going to do that?"

"You're the police; you've got a gun. Shoot them…."

"Good day sir, I'll file a report."

The Ward Boys

When some people move into a new neighborhood, they expect to bring their old one with them…Part 2

It was mid-May in 1979, around 1:00 PM on a Saturday in Lee, New Hampshire. The dispatcher had been very clear. "Get out there on the double."

The police chief flogged the Buick and arrived at the source of the call. He braked to a hard stop, throwing the transmission into park. The visual impact of the encounter caused him to hunch over the steering wheel, paralyzed, unable to move, incapacitated. Holding his head in his hands, breathing in spasms, gasping, his body shaking, tears rolled down his face. An electric orange 1972 Datsun pickup truck!

It was a common belief back then that whoever selected the colors for the Datsun company spent too much of their paycheck on LSD and not enough on nutrition.

My brother Ted's Datsun was typical of the Japanese pickups of the period, lightweight with tough mechanicals. Easy to drive and maintain. Cheap to operate and fix. Just fast enough to get you to Boston without getting killed. On the other hand, if you did wreck, you would be killed. When struck head on, they tended to fold up like a ham sandwich made with one piece of bread. If you were wearing your seatbelt, you became the ham.

The Datsun with a typical payload

But the real problem was "New Hampsha Cansa," ("Cancer" is pronounced "Cansa" in New Hampshire) which was the rust that arrived inevitably within 18 months of purchase. The brand and amount of rustproofing applied was immaterial. If a truck could be completely immersed in a vat of it and driven, it would still rust. Ground zero was the join of the fenders behind the front wheels. A thumb-sized paint blister today was a fist-sized hole in a month. Then with one solid pot hole hit, the fender bottom would detach from the body. It was a material failure that even duct tape could not fix.

From inside the vehicle, the wayward fenders created a speed-dependent symphony of high and mid-range fwapping, whirring, and tapping. The rhythm section for the ensemble was provided whenever a "road hazard" was encountered. Depending on the level of the sheet metal's decrepitude, the sound could be anything from a "whang" to a "boom". Since most late spring New Hampshire roads are by nature "road hazards," the rhythm section could be pretty loud. It was the Granite State "beatah", "shitbox", or insert your own invective, truck of the seventies. They didn't start that way; that's just how they devolved. This one was in the later stages of its devolution. It was finally traded in two years later to a dealership I worked at, fetching the princely sum of $200. I mean, after all, it ran.

Billy the lot-boy complained that it didn't have any brakes, pedal, or emergency. I gave him a look reserved for the mentally deficient and said, "Double clutch and downshift to stop. Then find a slight incline." I reached in the passenger footwell and handed him a brick with a rope attached. "As you nose up to it, grab the brick; hold open the door with your left foot. Sling the brick underneath the door behind the front wheel. If you miss, drag it back with the rope and try again. Works every time."

Billy was not pleased. The dealership GM was even less so. "Get that piece of shit off my lot," he barked.

The truck was so ugly that they made me and Billy push it around back out of sight. We couldn't even wholesale it. It went straight into the crusher at Madbury Metals.

Twenty-two years before, we'd moved into town from Brooklyn and became the "index of integration" as the only black family in the town and school district. Imagine if you would, a bald eagle flying over your house. You can't help but stop, stare, and point. And that's what it was like the first time we went to Dover, New Hampshire on a Friday afternoon. Traffic came to a screeching halt by Farnham's clothing store on Central Avenue at the Lower Square when we got out of the car. And indeed, they stopped, stared, and pointed.

Back then, Lee consisted primarily of dirt roads and had more cows than people. I'd been gone for a few years. Coming back, it seemed as though the people had finally gained the upper hand in the population battle. The only remaining constant was that we were still the only Black family in town.

One afternoon, my brother Ted and I were "checking out the changes in town." The sun was shining, and the temperature was in the mid 60's. Looking into the deep woods, you could still see the last remnants of snow. Here and there, the melt from the remaining snow piles meandered across the road. It was perfect weather for cruisin' with the windows down and the radio on. Not to mention holding a cold one between your thighs, so as not to advertise the fact. On the floor, the four remaining cans of a six pack of Shaefer sat in a paper bag. The AM radio chirped tinny Beatles songs, already "oldies" by then, as the truck growled along in 4th gear at 30 miles per hour. We were "backroadin'" in the best New Hampshire tradition.

We turned off Route 155 into a new development.

"Wow, they really did a number on Roger Woodhead's back pasture."

"I hear these houses are going for a quarter of a million dollars. I think that's the starting price."

"To live in Lee?"

"Well, there is the Oyster River School District for starters."

"Didn't know it was worth that much."

"It's worth what people will pay."

"It takes a fool and his money."

"Guess so."

"You want another?"

"Sure, crush this empty and put it behind the seat."

"Okay."

Coming to a stop sign, we turned the corner, and the truck began climbing up a small hill. From the opposite direction, the town police cruiser sailed over the top of it towards us at a high rate of speed. Holding our beers down below the level of the windows, we waved. The police chief stood on his brakes, pulled off the road and slid to a stop kicking up the gravel. He and I weren't particularly friendly, but it looked like he was smiling. Then we saw the oddest thing: he doubled over and rested his head on the steering wheel.

"Ted, is something wrong with him?"

"I have no idea, but if there is, he can call his own damn ambulance."

We continued on our way. No reason to look for trouble.

A month later, I dropped in to see Dad.

"Michael, were you and Ted cruising around James Farm on Saturday about a month ago?"

"Yeah, we were checking out the 'big money' houses."

"Well, dispatch got a 911 from some of the "new residents" up there. It seems that 'A pair of Blacks in an old truck are casing the neighborhood. We want them investigated, RIGHT NOW!'"

When dispatch asked for a status, all the chief could get out was "the Ward boys." He had to park his cruiser; he was laughing too hard to drive.

An Apology

The Rockingham Ballroom in Newmarket, NH was the site of the Oyster River High School Class of 1970's 30th Reunion. I was standing around slamming Buds with a bunch of guys. That's what Oyster River guys did in those days. In the meantime, my wife was spending quality time with some of my female classmates that she knew.

A "Queen Bee" female classmate came up to me, "Mike I really have to talk to you."

"Sure". This was odd; she was one of the girls who had stopped interacting with me in the 7th grade.

"Let's go over here, I don't want to be interrupted and I don't want anyone to hear this."

"Ok," What the hell?

"The only reason I came to this reunion was because I heard that you would be here. I don't really care about anybody else. The few friends I do have; we see each other when we want."

My internal alarm bells start to chime. I don't know what this is about, but the tingle says that it's not going to be good.

She continued. "My husband has served all over the world and down south with the military. I was shocked when I saw how black people are treated in this country. But I was completely humiliated when I realized what I had done to you. I locked myself in my bedroom and cried for hours."

The alarm bells are clanging now. This_is_not_a_drill...

"So, what did you do to me?"

"I made up stories about you, all the way from Junior High through High School."

"Ok, so?" Irritated now.

"I told the other girls at school not to go out with you. If they did, they wouldn't be invited to any parties. I even told you to stay away from my little sister, remember?"

Her father had threatened to put Dad out of business if I kept talking to or dancing with his youngest daughter. Harold had, in his own inimitable fashion, adjusted his medication. I was pretty drunk, and I was not ready for this.

"It probably won't do you much good to hear me say this, but if I could take it back I would. You're a nice, funny, handsome guy and you didn't deserve what I did to you."

The collision alert is howling in my brain. She's sitting less than two feet from me. I wanted to get up and walk away, wishing I'd never agreed to this. Electrocuted and welded to my chair, I can't. My body warps out, awaiting the signal from my brain. Reflexively, I begin to clench and unclench my fists. My pulse rising, banging in my head, traps and biceps swelling, legs and feet twitching, breath hissing, thinking to myself, "Smash the bitch."

"If I were you, I'd beat me up right here. You can pound me to a pulp, and I won't resist. I deserve it for what I did."

About to snap, barely keeping myself in check, choking, I could hardly breathe. This must be some kind of weird setup, where I lose it, punch her out, and get sued. I looked around the room. No one is even looking at us.

Then Dad spoke in my mind. *"No, Michael, you'll end up in jail and it won't solve anything."*

"You want me to forgive you?" I heard myself asking her, completely weirded out, collapsing internally.

"You don't have to if you don't want to, but I had to tell you what I did." Shattered with her admission, she blinked back tears.

"The damage is done. If my forgiveness will help you get through this, I forgive you." I sighed with resignation.

"What about you?"

"I'll survive. I always do."

Looking off, my soul had been vacuumed into a canyon of despair. I went to the bar, got a 16-ounce Bud, then went outside and stood on the walkway, alone. I wanted to scream and destroy something. But I couldn't. The code that Dad and

Mom had instilled in me was too powerful: *"Never let them see you hurt."*

Without thinking, I crushed the can; beer ran down my pants, tears formed in my eyes. I was afraid that I'd explode. I couldn't go back inside. Then shuddering, a primal panting of each word, just short of a scream:

"That_fucking_bitch_ruined_my_life."

Once again, I turned my back on my classmates. Looking up, I gazed at a sky full of August stars. I picked out the brightest, focusing, stressing out, channeling Whitesnake, singing without conscious thought.

"And here I go again..."

Crushed again, my voice locked up. My brother Ted had lived through the exact same hell.

A Sailor

It is a visual that would be recognized by a member of the Greatest Generation.

It is a visual that would be recognized by someone who had been in combat.

It is a visual that for many of us must be deduced, as a PTSD episode.

In mid-August of 2000 I was 48 years old. I had stopped in to see my parents. Mom was out for the evening.

Dad sat hunched over, stone silent, his face drawn tight, elbows on knees, gaze bore-sighted at the kitchen floor three feet in front of him. His eyes reflected horrors that had escaped from the vault in his memory that protected him from the past. A glass of Jack Daniels was held with both hands to keep it from shaking.

It was far too late in my life and after his ended that I understood the meaning of that pose. I remember seeing it first when Medgar Evers was killed. Then I saw it during the 1964 "Mississippi Burning" incident and at several other junctures over my lifetime. But I had never deciphered its significance. It was on that day after the Kursk, a Russian submarine was lost with 118 men undergoing sea trials, that I understood the pose, but not the name.

Among sailors there is no distinction between surface vessels or submarines, you are all men of the sea. And for a sailor, a ship does not sink. She dies, and often, her crew with it. Dad's anger and disgust with the Russian Government and Navy was monumental in proportion. But it was no less than what I remember as a young boy with the loss of the Thresher and her complement of 129, on her shakedown cruise out of Portsmouth in 1963.

"They keep sending them out for sea trials before they are ready. There's no reason for it, there's no war on. In the life of a boat, an extra week or month isn't going to matter. They keep showing off and killing us."

In the world of men at sea, there are always two enemies, the ocean and your adversary. In all cases your opponent is secondary. The ocean must be conquered first, before you can defeat your adversary.

It is this that my father understood.
It is this which rekindled his PTSD.
It is this that reduced him to tears and shaking hands, when the Kursk was abandoned by her Navy and her country.

For those who go down to the sea in ships,
It is thus.
When a ship dies, all sailors feel her loss.
And my father was a sailor.

Keep Your Money

My brother Ted possessed many complex character traits. The pair that best defined him, however, were not that complicated. His minimalism and directness were "Occam's Razor" personified. "Occam's Razor" is a principle from philosophy that gives precedence to simplicity: of two competing theories, the simpler explanation is preferred.

In Ted's case, his character was manifested as brilliant, terrifying, seductive and/or infuriating. He easily met or exceeded the Ward family standard for "hard headedness." Most members of the human race develop and refine facets of their personality over an extended period of time. Consider a three-year-old boy. Comparing his personality to an alcoholic spirit would be something akin to a Nouveau Beaujolais, thin, sweet, and unrefined. No so with Ted. By age three, he was already "barrel proof Wild Turkey."

In the mid-forties, older Black women in Brooklyn were into perfumes, furs, and blue hair tint. There was an equation at work here. The larger and homelier the woman, the more fur, perfumes, and blue tint were applied.

At three, Ted was a handsome and slender boy. On this day in 1945, in keeping with Mom's decree, he was "dressed to the nines." His hair was groomed, parted and Brylcreemed.

Perched on one of the best chairs in the living room, he awaited the arrival of one of Mom's friends.

Ted 1945

Even then, Ted had a discriminating eye for the ladies. On this day, unfortunately, beauty was not in the eyes of the beholder. The visitor in question was huge and elderly. If Rita Hayworth was a pinup queen, the visitor was the box that the magazine came in. Or to quote Dad, "She was as ugly as the back end of a truck."

She wore a fur stole of either chinchilla or mink. The tail of one hung down over her massive left breast. Its throat was stitched to the rump of its erstwhile kennel mate. Thus joined, the beasts crawled up over her breast to her shoulder. Not unlike a team of Sherpas roped together, as they ascended Everest's North Col. The Sherpas continued their march across the broad land bridge of her shoulders and back down across her right breast. There, the lead beast lay sprawled, head down, suspended over the edge of the abyss. Its stiff legs extended straight out in front of him, as if he were attempting to leap to his death.

She began her inexorable advance on Ted. The tail of the left-hand Sherpa wagged as she moved. On the right, the leader's head bobbed, his forelegs jerked sympathetically with each stride. With her decreasing proximity came an acute sense of asphyxiation from the semi-toxic combination of perfume and the industrial strength chemicals that were required to straighten her hair. This was, by the way, a shade of blue better known for its later appearance on the fenders of a 1955 Pontiac Star Chief coupe.

Now within striking distance, she leaned over him. The animal on the right took advantage of the laws of gravity by swinging suddenly towards his face. Its desiccated mouth was stitched shut in a linear snarl. The black glass eyes glared and glittered demonically at him.

She looked him over and chirped. "Ohhhhh, what a handsome little man, you're so cute!" Then she offered her cheek. "Can I have a kiss?"

"No," said Ted firmly.

Taken aback, but boring in again, chuckling conspiratorially, she countered, "I'll give you a nickel."

With total conviction, Ted replied, "Keep your money."

An Excellent Design

Virginia was the queen of all she surveyed in her living room. She reposed in a large green wing armchair that she had found at the dump and reupholstered. From this dais, pronouncements, declarations and judgments were rendered swiftly with unerring finality. Virginia "took no prisoners." Woe to the individual who failed to meet her expectations.

Virginia

On this day in February of 2008, the individual in question was her 60-something son, Ted. She was at her merciless best "Some engineer you are," she snorted with contempt.

"It's not my fault that the damn tape failed. I spent over two hours on it. It was an excellent design and did the job!"

"It did the job all right," she huffed dismissively.

He sulked...

Several Weeks Before

A tsunami of ice enveloped the state. Communication and
power lines lay on the ground, snapped like boxed linguini
before being thrown into a pot of boiling water. Total
darkness. To fly over New Hampshire at night that week was
a visual throwback to an era of "pre-electrification." In the
northern counties, the households were not as heavily
dependent on electricity. When the power goes out in a wood
heated house, so what?

But in the southern counties, woodstoves are less common.
Without one, you could, of course, enjoy some "indoor
winter camping." However, for a couple in their eighties, that
was not a viable option. Instead, they were evacuated from
their home and forced, to quote Blanche Dubois, "to depend
on the kindness of strangers." That was Dad and Mom's
plight. They moved to the home of a friend with a generator
until power was restored.

Upon returning home a week later, they found that although
power had been restored, there was no water coming from
the well. The well was about 40 feet from the side door of
their house below grade in a tiny shed. Inside, a three-foot
section of PVC pipe ran from the well head to the
underground inlet that fed the house. Normally, a
thermostatically actuated switch triggered a 100-watt bulb

that warmed the exposed section of pipe. Ensuring that the bulb could maintain a temperature above freezing throughout a New Hampshire winter where -30 degrees is not unheard of, required insulation. The internal roof and walls were completely encased in foil faced R24 insulation, and the seams were tightly taped.

A week of sub-20-degree weather and no electricity caused an ice plug to form in the inlet to the house from the pump. Left to its own devices, it wouldn't thaw by itself until spring. Neither a heat lamp nor tape could thaw the underground section of the pipe. Dad sighed in frustration.

"Ted, the damn inlet's frozen."

"Wait, I've got an idea."

And as country people do, Ted improvised and made it work. He disconnected the PVC link from the pump to the inlet. Then with cardboard, aluminum foil, and duct tape, a cone was fabricated around the end of the inlet. A 1500-watt heat gun, retailing for $29.99 from the Black & Decker outlet store in Kittery, Maine, was duct taped to a clamp. That, in turn, was attached to one of the roof supports. Thus secured, it was locked on "high" and focused on the center of the cone. The jet of superheated air that was force fed down the pipe slowly began to melt the ice plug.

After some "fine tuning," Ted monitored his invention for about 10 minutes. Then he went inside the house. Why sit in a frigid 4'x4' box watching a pipe thaw?

Mom, Dad, and Ted sat around the kitchen for a comfortable hour or so talking. Mom was sipping Sambuca and brandy. The men were "touching" some bourbon. Then Ted saw the time. That universal human experience, love, that ensnares almost every one of us at one time or another, asserted itself in a spectacular manner.

Ted had a date that evening with a new lady friend. Between the pump and the bourbon, he'd lost track of time. "Jesus, I've gotta get out of here."

Grabbing his hat and coat, he bolted out of the house, into his truck, and down the road. Unfortunately, the calming effect of the libations made him forget why he was there in the first place. It was at this point that, to borrow an analogy from Monopoly, things went:

"Straight to hell."
"They did not pass 'Go.'"
"They did not collect $200."

The heat rose steadily inside the tiny super-insulated building. As it did, the duct tape adhesive warmed and relaxed. The gravity and the thrust from the heat gun took care of the rest. Slowly, it pivoted until the blast of superheated air hit a wooden component of the structure. With the building designed to hold heat, all of the material inside was thoroughly preheated and dried before it ignited. The asphalt shingles that sheathed the exterior became an oven enclosure. The roof was breached when the fire could no longer be contained. A mini-Vesuvius spewed flames and ash into the night sky. Finally, the sides caved into the well hole. So complete was the cycle of self-immolation that there was almost nothing left to take to the transfer station.

A phenomenon exists that is unique to country life. A building can catch fire at night, burn completely to the ground, and no one will notice it until the next day. And that is exactly what happened. The next morning, Dad and Mom awoke to find not only that was there still no water, but also that there was no pump house either.

Lance Corporal Beverly Theodore Ward USMCR never lived it down.

Overwatch

Dedicated to Joe Schanda and the "Band of Brothers" from American Legion Post #67 in Newmarket, New Hampshire.

The horseshoe-shaped driveway in front of the house was ringed by massive white pines. The late February ice storm had been startling in its ferocity. The ice had layered on inexorably until the tree limbs, some the size of a horse's thigh, could take no more. Their natural defense, flexion, failed them after they became entombed. Signaling surrender with sharp cracks, not unlike gunshots, one by one they came to earth. Their natural symmetry lost as they speared the ground, interlocking and frozen into a massive sprawl.

When it was over, the yard was a scene of utter devastation. The power and phone lines were down. There was no danger of electrocution; the wires had been ripped from the poles. The driveway was impassable. My brother Ted drove across the lawn to get to the house.

Entering the house late that afternoon, it was dark, cold, and quiet. In the kitchen, the gas oven was on at 550 degrees. With the door open, it provided the only heat in the house. Our parents sat by it in the semi-dark, quietly drinking tea. Mom's was "assisted" with brandy.

"We were wondering when you'd show up."

Ted loaded Mom and Dad and a pair of overnight bags into his pickup. Then he brought them to my house.

After the storm was over, Joe Schanda, a member of Legion Post 67 in Newmarket, drove up to Lee to check on Mom and Dad. After seeing the condition of the yard, he mobilized the post. They called my house to say that they'd be cleaning up the yard that Saturday.

The previous Thanksgiving, Dad had left their church one evening to warm up the Ford. He slipped on the ice and fell while opening the car door. His right leg slid underneath the rocker panel. Since he held on to the door to keep from falling, his femur became the pivot point. It snapped. He was in no shape to do any kind of outdoor activity. So it was game on for Ted and me.

Hard cold, the early afternoon sun was a heatless afterthought. The men worked in silence, cutting, hacking, dragging, and lifting. Occasionally, the snarl of a chainsaw would rip the silence, but for the most part, it was quiet. A fellow and his tractor had shown up earlier in the day. Using the front-end loader and a chain, he had broken up some of the larger heaps. But both the tractor and its owner had retreated to a warmer location.

The north wind whickered down through the trees, slowly crawling over them, indolent and condescending. It caressed the planes of their faces like a frozen straight razor. The exhalation of their breaths slithered sideways, as if afraid to rise. Pinched faces, narrowed eyes, and reddened ears with white-tinged edges of incipient frostbite. Every now and again, hands would be placed in armpits to halt the tingling of fingers.

I turned to Ted. "It's too cold for this shit. Why don't we just clear part of the driveway and wait until spring?"

"I'm not disagreeing with you, but these old men fought through worse than this in the war. They aren't complaining, so we sure can't."

It was true.

"Jesus, those tree limbs look like those damn German tank traps when we got caught in that mess at Bastogne. Just as fucking cold too. You remember that one, don't you Joe?"

Joe chuckled; "No way. I was in the Navy. We had our own problems."

"Yeah, you did."

He looked off to the distance. Then his face sagged as his mind replayed something he never wanted to see again. He began shaking, but not from the cold. Tears began to form and freeze on his face. "Dammit, those bastards almost got us all."

Joe grabbed his arm. "Let it go; you made it."

Another man approached. Joe jerked his head in the first man's direction. "You were in the Army with him. He needs somebody."

Nodding, the other man grabbed the first man's arm. He quietly walked him away from the group.

"You have to move on from that stuff. It'll kill you if you don't. For Chrissakes, that was more than sixty years ago, he's still hanging on to it."

"Joe, we're all still hanging on…"

With few exceptions, none of the men clearing the shattered trees from Dad's yard was less than 65 years old. "Buckle down. Get it done." The cold didn't matter. They had endured and come home from much, much worse, Guadalcanal, Bastogne, Frozen Chosin.

Dad wasn't a Newmarket High grad. He was a black Navy World War II veteran from New York City. For half of his career he had served in segregated rates. But in the silent understanding of former men at arms, he was their "brother," and dammit, they took care of their own.

Old Glory

Old Glory whipped, buffeted and bellowed her authority. Suspended on her pole in the backseat of the red Mustang convertible, she spoke her defiance into the 70 mph wind.

An Hour Earlier

It was 80 degrees at the 2009 Memorial Day parade in Lee, New Hampshire. The light blue sky was clear and cloudless. The sun splashed anything that could reflect it. Those things that couldn't reflect absorbed its light and displayed their hues in a vivid palette. Musical instruments, flags, motor vehicles, horses, uniforms, and people, all radiating in a visual harmony that was felt as much as seen. But with Lee being a small town, the parade took all of forty-five seconds to pass in review. It ended at the town's War Memorial.

At the ceremony, a member of the American Legion sang the National Anthem. The crowd nodded their silent assent when he finished.

A Lt. Colonel from the Army was the speaker. He spoke of the ideals that had led the citizens being memorialized to place themselves in "harm's way" and not return. He spoke of sacrifices that they didn't want to make but were made to preserve the right for their nation, their town and their loved ones to live and prosper. He finished with, "It was their sacrifice that allows us to stand here today, safe, unafraid, and free…"

A wreath was placed on a stand beside the memorial by the parade's Grand Marshal, Harold E. Ward, Petty Officer 1st Class, USN Ret. (Purple Heart Guadalcanal), and Lewis Henry Spec4 USA (Purple Heart, Vietnam).

Harold and Lewis

The two men held their salutes as the Sargent of the revolutionary war reenactor detail barked a command. The six-pounder cannons affirmed his order with a sharp crack; when the gunpowder ignited it fed a deep baritone hammer boom. Three volleys were called, and with each, clouds of gunsmoke wafted over the crowd. It was a sharp, acrid, angry scent, foreign to most, but all too familiar to the few.

The Lt. Colonel thanked everyone for coming. Then the crowd of neighbors, relatives and visitors began to mingle, conversing as they milled around the memorial and the cannons. After a while the crowd began to disperse.

Dad had been picked up at home by the owner of the mid Sixties Chrysler convertible that was his ride for the ceremony. But afterwards the owner hustled up to Northwood to be in their parade.

That left the Parade's Grand Marshal with no ride home. He was about to start thumbing when Alan Knight Corporal, USMC (Vietnam) said, "Hey Harold, you want a ride?"

"Sure."

They walked over to Alan's red Mustang convertible, "Harold. it's a nice day, you mind if I leave the top down?"

"No, that'd be great." Dad climbed into the car and buckled up. He took off his VFW 10676 Post Commander's "fore and aft" hat and put it on his lap.

American Legion Post 67 in Newmarket, New Hampshire had lent their American flag for the parade. It was Alan's job to return it to the post. He stood holding it for a minute, deciding. Then he looked at Dad sitting in the front seat and thought. "The hell with it".

He unfurled Old Glory and put the base of her pole on the floor in the back seat. He then secured the pole tightly with cross hatched backseat belts. "There, that oughtta do it."

The Mustang grumbled down Mast Road past the school, the church, the cemetery and the town offices. Alan hung a left off Mast onto Lee Hook Road past the Grange hall, still rolling at a stately 30mph. But after dropping down over the brow of the hill onto the flat, Alan gave her the spurs and let the Mustang run.

In her front seats rode two men who were totally unalike. They were veterans of different colors, different generations, and different wars. Yet they were bonded by having lived through events where survival is a random construct. It is a bond that over time fewer people in this country understand, and even fewer share. And after looking death in the eye at the bequest of their country, they were brothers.

Alan and Harold sat stretched out in the front seats. They were grinning from ear to ear like a pair of young kids at the fair. They reveled and basked in the sunlight and the 70mph breeze. From the backseat, Old Glory roared her thanks to them for protecting her and obliterated any thought of conversation.

They rode like this for two miles, over the Lamprey River, up the hill, through the Hook and up the hill to Harold's house. Seventy is 30 mph over the posted speed limit, but Alan didn't care.

"We fought for this flag. We earned this ride. No cop in this state would ever pull us over."

And none did.

Titanium Rose

Definitions:

Rose: A woody perennial flowering plant of the genus Rosa or the flower it bears. They form a group of plants that are often armed with sharp prickles.

Titanium (Ti): a lustrous transition metal with a silver-gray color, low density, and high strength.

Virginia Elizabeth (White) Ward was my mother. She had been smoking since age 15. When she was 86, she developed lung cancer. The radiation used to kill it destroyed her lungs. Over time her respiratory function diminished. Her last eight months were spent in a slow downward spiral. But assisted by her oxygen exchanger, she had proudly made it to her 89th birthday on August 2nd.

But now it was the middle of October. Dad had stressed out over her condition and not been taking care of himself. He ended up in a short-term rehab facility to get revitalized. Until then, Mom had been humming along at home with him. But she couldn't be left to tend herself, so she was moved into the Hyder House Hospice at the Strafford County Complex in Dover, New Hampshire for a short-term stay while Dad recovered.

At this point Mom had achieved that stasis that medical professionals marvel about. She was supposed to be dead. But Virginia, forever the contrarian, was not.

The previous week, the "Lee Plant Thugs" had come by the house. These were the women that ran the Plant booth at the town fair with her for 40 years. Mom was established as the "African Violet Queen" of the Lee Fair. The Plant Thugs took her out for a spin around all the roads in Lee in a hired limousine with chilled champagne. She came back boosted, positive, and happy. Then she checked into Hyder House. I sat with her that afternoon. She looked out the window across a field and into the surrounding woods. "This is a nice place."

I saw her again the next day. But this time when we looked out the window it was snowing. Snow on October 21st! She said nothing about it, but she seemed to deflate. The sight of it meant having to endure yet another New Hampshire winter while in declining health. Unbeknownst to me and the rest of the family, she decided to pull the plug.

It was several days before I saw her again. This time on my way to her room, her nurse, a young woman, pulled me aside, "She's going, it won't be long now." This startled me. I went into her room. She was no longer the person that I had laughed and joked with days prior. She lay unmoving, mute. My mother was dying.

"Hi Mom! It's Mike." I said this loudly because, for the dying, hearing is the last of the senses to fail.

She gasped, "Mahk…"

"Would she say anything more?" I wondered and waited for several moments. No, just that single expulsion of breath and silence. She lay on her side and stared back at me sightlessly. Her face was thin and drawn, but not wrinkled. I smiled as the thought, "If you're black you don't crack" slipped into my mind.

That dynamic silvery gray bun, the crown that she had always pulled her hair back into was no longer. Now it was a loose assemblage of exhausted, frizzled, limp white strands, splayed listlessly on her head. Her irises were deep dark, bottomless pools. Whatever she saw was no longer of this earth and beyond my grasp. Her breathing was slow and measured, almost as if she was saving her strength. That full radiant, vibrant smile, the sharp quip, mellow laugh, and dancing eyes, were now only memories.

Without warm-up I sang one of her favorite songs, "A Bridge over Troubled Water." When I reached into the upper registers, the ones that I used to rip through with total abandon in my twenties, I took it easy. But when I got to the last verse, I dialed it up. Ever the showman, I didn't care who heard me. I was in a hospice dammit. "The people in here are going to die. If today is their day, they won't enter that long good night in silence if I can help it."

I bounced my voice off the ceiling. I belted the last chorus, primal and raw. The emotional stress and over-singing caused my voice to crack in the last two lines. I ignored it and powered through. I gave my mother all that I had and that's all that counted. And then for the only time in fifty years, tears came.

I stood up, leaned over, and put my hand on her shoulder. "I love you Mom. Thanks for putting up with me. It couldn't have been easy, but I made it. Brian, Rachie and all of your great grandchildren are doing great. Don't worry about Dad; we'll take care of him. We're all going to miss you. It's time for you to say hello to Grand mom Elzena and little brother Brucie. Goodbye Momma." I kissed her on her lips.

I left the room dazed. My body was ringing from the exertion of singing, but now minus half of its life's source. I walked past the nurse's station.

"Excuse me sir. Was that you singing?" The same nurse as before asked me quietly.

I stopped, "Yes. I'm sorry. Was I too loud?"

"No, it was beautiful, lovely."

"Thank you. It was her favorite song. I just wanted to make sure she heard me."

"I'm sure she did. I like your mother. I talked to her before…, she paused and then continued. "She was a sweet, sweet lady. I'm glad that you spent time with her. A lot of people come in here and don't interact or spend time with their relatives. They act like they're afraid of them. It's as if they're checking a box on a form or something. They just go in, look and then leave as fast as they can. You're a good son." Her eyes were blinking rapidly. It was only then that I realized she was crying too.

Then we stood, two total strangers, and held each other for several moments. After releasing our embrace, we stepped away, back into our own separate worlds.

The "Titanium Rose" in Dad's fisted glove, left us a day later on October 25th, 2009. It was exactly one week shy of her and Dad's 64th wedding anniversary. She was 89 years old.

A Lifetime Crush

A true friendship is a bond that spans ages; nor does it fade over time and distance.

As a child growing up in Lee and going to Mast Way Elementary School, Susan Wellington was captivated by my father Harold Ward, the school janitor. He was a tall brown skinned man with a ready smile and booming laugh. Whenever possible she engaged him in conversation. And as was his habit when he dealt with children, he treated her in as much of an adult manner as possible. He spoke to her and answered her questions truthfully. Over time they forged a friendship that transcended their ages. Or in Harold-speak, "She was one of his kids."

Susan chose a career as an anthropologist. She has tended to live in faraway places such as Alaska and Australia. Every couple of years though, she cycles back through town. The last time was around 2013. She and her mother stopped in to see Harold. He was in the kitchen by the stove when they walked in. He looked up at her initially with a puzzled expression.

"Who is this?" And then he realized: "Oh My God, its Susan!"

When she was a child he towered over her. Shrunken now with age and three bilateral "total hip" replacements, the situation was reversed. Her height was now a conservative 6 feet, taller than most people.

They hugged. The bond between a 91-year-old man and a woman of 55 was elemental and total in its sincerity. She enveloped him in her arms, her long blonde hair completely covering his head and face. They stood, holding each other, not speaking for a long time. Her mother and I stood by, mute as a pair of salt and pepper shakers waiting on a table.

Then they stood apart, holding each other's hands. Both blinking back tears as they realized that this could be the last time they spoke. Their sentences ran together.

"I'm so glad you stopped in."

"I had to see you."

The conversation meandered on, neither of them wanting it to end.

After they left, he laughed and shook his head. "She came by to see an old goat like me."

Brotherhood

The brotherhood is passed down through generations.
An unbroken chain of red, white, & blue links.
Forged from the strongest material on earth.
Faith.
Faith in country.
Faith in purpose.
Faith in the brotherhood that is the tip of the United States
spear.

Final Salute

The combined American Legion and VFW ceremony at visiting hours at Kent and Pelzcar's Funeral Home in Newmarket, New Hampshire on June 12, 2015 had ended.

The line of Veterans stood silently, some blinking back tears as they prepared to extend their condolences.

The man was in his eighties, a former officer. He was still tall and firm but bent with the weight of age. He held my hand with both of his and wept.

"Your father was a good man. My God, I'm going to miss him. Please keep in touch."

Alan Knight, my UNH classmate, a grunt in Vietnam, had tears sliding down his cheeks. He knelt at the casket, unconsciously clenching and unclenching his fist.

"When we came home, nobody understood what we'd been through. They didn't want to hear it. Nobody gave a damn about us.

"I'd go to Exeter, over to Harold's bar. Sometimes he and I would just sit, not saying a word. Sometimes we'd talk for hours. If I didn't have any money, he'd just give me a beer. Cause he knew. He knew..."

Sea Change

The U.S. Navy sent a detail of two active duty sailors from the Portsmouth Naval Shipyard to bury Dad.

The bugler was a female E5. The crisp palette presented by her closely cropped red hair, sharply pressed summer whites, navy blue insignia, gold bugle, and black spit-shined shoes was startling in its precision and correctness.

The black sailor presenting the flag was an E6, Dad's rank. He was no less precise and perfectly turned out in summer whites.

Neither of those sailors existed in the segregated Navy of CS1 Harold E. Ward. Women weren't allowed into the Navy band until 1980. After boot camp, he was billeted as a "Mess Attendant/Steward." He was a U.S. Navy "employee" with no rank and paid less than a white sailor. Once they were deployed, Black sailors were not allowed to handle ammunition unless they were supervised. Handling a weapon under any circumstances was considered a court martial offense. Dad's "General Quarters" post was "stretcher bearer."

Until the day he died, June 9th, 2015, at 94 years of age, he cursed the Navy's usurpation of his right to fire a shot at the enemy. The denial of his being able to avenge the loss of friends at Pearl Harbor and in the 3rd Battle of Savo Island, was unforgiveable.

The bugler finished playing "Taps."

The E6 and I locked eyes. As he handed me Dad's flag he intoned, "On behalf of the President of the United States and a grateful nation, we sincerely regret your loss and present you this flag as a token of our appreciation."

A loud humming noise entered my consciousness, almost drowning out his words. By the end of his recitation, it had faded to almost nothing. Was Harold speaking to me one last time?

When the sailor finished, his eyes flickered, his jaw clenched ever so slightly, and with an imperceptible nod, he saluted.

He knew of the sacrifices of the Mess Attendants and the later integration of the military that had breached the barrier of institutionalized racism.

His presence before me was a testament to the success of individual endeavor, unbound by arbitrary constraints.

A torpedoman.

A warrior.

We Would Indeed

The ultimate expression of respect is love. When we moved to New Hampshire, Dad had no white friends.

The V8 grumbled as the truck thumped and jumped down the dirt road. It rebounded harshly out of some of the deeper washouts. It had been quite a while since I had traversed this stretch. What, forty years?

The road ended in a 'Y' with a homestead in the middle. A heavy duty 4x4 gleamed on the left branch, while an "experienced" SUV graced the right. It was a white clapboard, single-story dwelling, now well into its second century. Time revealed the bottom course of clapboards, as grey as a beard of a man a third of its age. Forty years ago, the addition sprouting to the right of the house was a stand of birch trees.

After shutting off the engine, it was quiet in the yard. No people. No dog or cats. Then, I heard the soft bleating of a young lamb, a sound of the country. It was coming from behind the 4x4. For the first time, I noticed an awning rising behind and above it.

A young woman appeared. She was tall; taut of body, and economical of movement. Studying each other, we were familiar and yet we were not. Transposition: I looked like my father, she like her mother.

Stepping forward, I saw a pair of young girls under the awning beside a pair of lambs on shearing stands. The shearing looked perfect.

"Darn it." Apparently, I was mistaken.

The other girl laughed.

Turning to the woman, "I'd like to see your mom please."

"She's with the boys in the house."

We walked across the grass to the addition. I told her that I took early retirement to take care of my father during his final weeks.

"Dad adored you folks. He loved babysitting you guys as kids."

"We loved him too."

"Yeah, a lot of people did. Thanks."

We stepped across the threshold into the house. Two little boys were scuffling around. I gave her mother a hug. Then I presented her with some photographs, a red plush comforter, and a brief note from my father.

"When it's cold and blustery, gather your daughter and the little ones together. When you wrap yourselves in this comforter, you'll be in Harold's arms."

"That's so sweet. Call me if you need help washing, cleaning, moving, anything." Her eyes were blinking rapidly. At the reception after Dad's service, I sensed the same loneliness in her that I felt.

All of her neighbors of 40 years prior for a mile in either direction on the main road were now gone. She had been a single mother for at least that long. My folks had been happily married for just shy of 64 years when my Mom passed in 2009. Ever since then, Dad had been living alone with his memories in his house up on the main road and pining for companionship.

"Take care." I walked back to my truck and got in.

Then she was at the passenger side window, struggling. "You know, your dad was special."

Time froze, I heard the same humming in my mind as when the sailor handed me Dad's flag. My visit today had been subconsciously triggered. I hadn't even considered what I said next. But when your heart is torn open, the truth will emerge. I had one shot at saying this right. "He loved you, you know. If his heart had been in better shape, you two would have been an item."

Looking down, she stiffened, stunned. Then she raised her head with pride, a smiling with a bit of sadness, but then speaking with absolute conviction.

"Yes. Yes, we would indeed."

A Place in the Sun

Dad had been interviewed by National WWII Museum oral historian Tom Gibbs. Tom was on a mission to capture Dad's story for the permanent oral history collection at the museum. His interview eventually made its way into the museum's "Road to Tokyo" gallery, which recounts the story of the Pacific war.

Dad spoke up because he felt that the injustice that he and his fellow Mess Attendants endured should not be whitewashed into the decks of U.S. Navy history. His further inclusion in the exhibits "The Roads to Berlin" and "Fighting for the Right to Fight" was due, in part, to the dichotomy that his service represented. "A sailor who was willing to bear arms in defense of his country but denied that opportunity by regulations that would punish him if he did."

The interview about his wartime experience was long and eloquent. It was more than three hours of vintage Harold: entertaining, precise and arresting.

Before he passed, Dad had asked that we attend the opening ceremony of "The Road to Tokyo" exhibit in his stead if he was no longer able. On December 11, 2015, my wife Donna, our son Brian and I honored his wish at the National WWII Museum in New Orleans. We crossed the glass bridge from the visitor center into the exhibit. And there he was on a video screen to our left.

Harold at the National WWII Museum

Once inside the exhibit, lifting a handset, seeing him on the video screen, and hearing him speak once more was indescribable.

After the opening ceremony, Brian systematically checked out every item on the shelves of the gift shop looking for some reference to Harold's service. He was observed by Daniel Martinez, the chief historian of the USS Arizona Memorial for the National Park Service. He approached Brian in the café.

"I used to teach high school. I know intensity in young people when I see it. I saw you going through the gift shop. What are you looking for?"

"I was looking for something about my grandfather's service in the war."

He looked at Brian's name tag. "Are you by chance related to Harold Ward?"

"Yes, he was my grandfather."

Donna added, "He was my father-in-law and his son Mike is over at that table

"I am so glad to meet you. We've been looking for you all week. Harold's interview is important because the Mess Attendants were too ashamed of their service to come forward and speak about it at length. His interview was so complete and concise that it is the reference history of a Mess Attendant's service in World War II. I'm sorry that I never had a chance to meet him."

We were surprised to find out that he knew who Dad was. It was even more humbling to find out that people were searching the audience for us. "We really appreciate what you've told us. We're really moved that you would try to find us." I had an original draft of Sketches of Lee with me, so I gave it to him. He browsed through it and was impressed.

"Thank you. This is really well done. But we're not finished with you yet. You'll be getting something very special in the mail very soon."

In early February 2016, I received a large envelope in the mail from the U.S. Government. The enclosed decree from President Barack Obama, enshrined the career of CS 1 Harold Emanuel Ward, USN, as part of the official history of the United States of America.

The United States of America
honors the memory of

Harold E. Ward

This certificate is awarded by a grateful nation in recognition of devoted and selfless consecration to the service of our country in the Armed Forces of the United States.

President of the United States

Mr. Daniel Martinez, on behalf of Harold's and Virginia's "United Nations" of seven grandchildren and nine great-grandchildren, I thank you.

American Hero: The Bus Company Owner

On Saturday, July 16, 2016, I was the master of ceremonies at Lee, New Hampshire's 250th anniversary celebration. Starting at 10:00 a.m. I announced a 45-element parade of over 80 vehicles, floats, horses, bands, random people, and farm animals. During the breaks between my announcing duties, I fronted for the original omnibus copy of my book, Sketches of Lee, at the information booth.

It was 4:00 p.m. The canopy topping the booth was being ignored by the late afternoon sun slanting in from the west. Laterally enveloped by a wall of full spectrum light and radiant heat, I felt like a chicken on a rotisserie spit. Artificial hip and all, I had been standing in the sun for over six hours.

A man in his late thirties or early forties approached the booth. Introducing myself, I explained that I had written a book about my family's experience in Lee. We chatted as he browsed through a copy I handed him.

"Are you from Lee?"

"Yes, I'm Peter Gibb."

"Are you related to Roger Gibb?"

"He was my grandfather."

I looked at him. "I mentioned him in a story."

"Wow, I'll have to buy a copy. How much are they?"

"Twenty dollars, but since I spoke of your grandfather in a positive light, it's free."

"Well, I don't take things without paying."

"You can't pay me enough."

"I'll give you $50."

"No."

"Then I'll give you $10."

"Don't be insulting, it's free."

In the meantime, his wife, daughter, and son have wandered over. She looked at him quizzically. "Why is he arguing with the event master of ceremonies?"

"He won't let me pay for his book."

Mrs. Gibb looked at me as if I'm crazy. By now, most of the crowd had left. It was not as if I was doing a land-office business. This was frustrating. The man couldn't take a hint. But as matter of principle, I could not take his money either.

"Look, let me read you the story." As I said it, I looked at his family. The boy was a gangly six-foot 15-year-old. He could handle it. Beside him stood his 11-year-old sister with a shy smile, her light brown hair flowing in waves down to midback, askew from a day in the sun. She stood leaning back, her head nestled against her mom's shoulder. It was the classic daughter and mother expression of mutual adoration and pure love, unsullied by the storm of teenage years lurking just over the horizon.

I had a moment of panic and indecision. I stressed, wondering, "Should I do this?" Then I resolved. "Her parents will talk her through it."

I begin: "An American Hero, a Regular Guy." The story rolled off my lips as I painted a canvas of autumnal beauty and youthful innocence.

Pausing for a split second, I thought, "Could I do an on-the-fly rewrite?" That wasn't going to cut it. Steeling my courage now, apologizing in my mind. "I'm really sorry, little girl, but this is going to hurt."

The "N word" leapt off the page and struck the family like a four-headed cobra. Visceral, they recoiled in unison. But once past that point, I was all in, powering on, almost bold. I was confident that the horror of those wretched words would ultimately be slain by two men who saw "kids as kids."

From "An American Hero, a Regular Guy"

Roger Gibb, the bus company owner, said, "Nobody has the right to abuse the kids on my buses."

And the school board agreed.

I finished. "That's why you can't pay me for the book. Your grandfather paid for it 50 years ago".

Roger Gibb's grandson, granddaughter-in-law, great-grandson, and great-granddaughter stood as statues, mute. For the first time, they learned that the battle for civil rights in America wasn't just a "southern thing." Their late patriarch was an unsung hero in that fight. In 1961, he and Gerard Doucette stood shoulder to shoulder, standing firm in the belief that "that all men and women are created equal."

Mr. Gibb's eyes widened, and he spoke softly, "I never heard that story before."

"Well, I had to tell it to you. I always read stories to people if they or their relatives are included."

I shook his hand. The boy stood frozen, his pupils dilated, but in them I could see a glimmer of pride. His mom's expression was set, her emotions in check. The daughter looked a little unsteady, as if she had jumped from a skiff onto land after riding in four foot swells. There would be a discussion at the Gibbs dinner table that night.

Transformed, they turned to leave

As a family

No longer oppressed by the heat of the day

Aglow with a testament to the strength of their lineage

Of which they had been totally unaware

As a family

Visibly uplifted

Proud, standing tall

Close enough to touch

As a family
Walking away together

A New Hampshire Moment

On September 9, 2017, I worked a booth at the Lee Fair from 11:00 AM until 7:00 PM. It seemed fitting to introduce the first volume of my Sketches of Lee collection, A Colored Man in Exeter, at the fair. Foot traffic was light. I passed out a bunch of handbills but did not make too many sales.

The town library had a copy. VFW Post 10676 received its copy (from Harold) at the fair. However, the VFW brotherhood went online after their Wednesday meeting and ordered a bunch. Since the word is finally out in town, I feel its "Mission Accomplished."

It was sunset. As I was leaving the fair, I saw Police Chief Tom Dronsfield. He had been a patrolman back when Dad was on the force. He had worked his way up, finally achieving the rank of chief. Dad revered him. When it was time for that last ambulance ride, Dad was adamant. He refused to leave. His voice was not strong, but his resolve was. "I want to die in my own bed."

No amount of persuasion from the ambulance, police, or fire services could convince him to leave his home of 58 years. Most of the first responders had known him for decades, some as infants. Slowly Dad's stubbornness took its toll. Anyone who didn't need to be inside the house wasn't. Instead, they stayed outside on the lawn. Some stood, looking away from the house. Others looked at the ground, their tears falling and melting into the earth. The patrolman realized that unless the stalemate was broken, the first responders would no longer be able to function. As a last resort, the patrolman radioed for assistance.

Tom drove to the house, went in, and gave it to his friend directly. "Harold, there are only two ways you can leave your house, head first or feet first. As your friend, I'd feel much better if you left head first."

"Ok, Chief, I'll go."

Stopping the truck, I got out. Looking up at the sky, I said to Tom, "It's sunset--a good time to read this story. 'The Kitchen Is Closed.'"

Then a New Hampshire moment.

In the twilight of a late summer day.

A white cop and a black man.

Standing beside State Road 155.

Two men, eyes wet, hugged.

This was Harold's life work, exemplified.

Two years on, he was still bringing people together.

I bid you peace.

Bonded Through Eternity

There are some life stories that simply cannot be made up. This is one of them.

Olivia and Matthew Egan met Dad on Thanksgiving Day 2012. In age they were respectively 3, 2, and 91 years old. They spent the next two Thanksgiving holidays together. They only knew each other for two and a half years before he passed, but in that short time, Olivia in particular took a liking to him. She decided that she "loved" him. As for Dad? He was just as taken by them as they were with him.

When he was in his final decline, their mother, Jodi, would bring them to the hospital to visit him every week. Olivia would wear clothes that she thought "Harold would like." Dad would be lying in his hospital bed, connected to a drip, oxygen, and a monitoring cuff. Then Matthew and Olivia would climb all over him like he was a jungle gym. He loved it.

During one visit, they were tussling and in a contentious mood. They simply could not be reined in. Jodi was mortified. She asked me to apologize to Dad about it.

"What for? They were fine. They're just little kids burning off steam."

Before Dad's wake, Olivia and Matthew took his message to heart, his story about giving new babies a silver dollar. "So they can start life with some money in their pocket."

At the wake, they had Jodi slide two silver dollars into the pocket of his Navy jumper. Olivia proclaimed, "After waiting so long to see Virginia, once he gets to heaven, he'll need some money to take her out dancing."

A few days afterwards, Jodi asked her how she was feeling. "I miss Harold, but it's okay. He's with Virginia now. He's happy to be with his true love."

This was from a five-year-old. Several months later, she declared, "Harold is my guardian angel."

Then I received this from Jodi. "Some days that blonde bombshell gives me heartburn, but when she talks about Harold, she melts my heart. I can't explain the connection this little blond girl had to your Dad, but I love it and find it to be so cool. It makes me feel like we as parents did something so right!

"Every year we buy helium balloons on her birthday. She knows which balloon she's sending Harold before we even pay for it. I promise, I do not prompt her to do this in any way. She just does it. And she wants to do it. I've attached a picture of this year's balloon, 'Going to find Harold!'"

Over his lifetime, Dad "adopted" many young people. But the spontaneous and solid bond created between Olivia, Matthew, and him was unprecedented. They were his last adopted "Ward kids." And as his representative on earth, I will love and watch over these little ones forever.

Olivia sending a balloon to Harold

Reunited

It was warm that morning.

The sky?
Light blue
A crystal clarity flowing forever
Upwards to the sun.

We stood
It was neither a large nor heavy box
"Do you want to do it?"
"Sure."

Kneeling on the grass
Realizing
I would have to lie on my stomach.

Looking down inside
A slight gleam at the bottom
Made me smile.

Reaching down
Fully extending my arms
Lowering the box
I couldn't touch the bottom.

Worming forward
Another foot
Head and shoulders
Down inside.

A vision of being pulled out
Feet first
I smiled.
Stretching…

A soft "thump"
A granite box of ashes
Now resting at the foot of the coffin

"Mom, your baby boy is with you
Goodbye, big brother."

Limitless Blue

Rising
Dusting off my pants
Reaching back
Into my hip pocket.

Condensation
Making it slippery
Finally
Cold in my hand.

"I'll split a Bud with you"
I pounded half
The rest, on the grass
"Bye Teddie!"

Now, by my feet
On the headstone
Next to the flowers
Standing at attention.

A "4th of July" Budweiser
A Marine's last beer.

Looking up
Searching
A cloud
A bird
A rainbow

A sign.

Nothing

A warm limitless blue silence.
He was truly gone.

A Single Tree

The Ward men
Of my generation and above
Are gone

Bruce
Ted
And Harold.

All residing
In the same metaphysical space of eternity
But I remain.

I can no longer look right or left
For assistance
Guidance
Or humor
I can only look upward.

Waiting by the grave for the benediction
Dad spoke for the final time

As leaves
Their bottoms
Upturned to the sun
Crackling
Hissing
Twisting in the wind.

It is a tongue that I will not understand

Until it's my turn.

Forever,
May loved ones remain
In our hearts.

Ted 2010

As beacons
Ever onward
Charting our course.

Virginia and Harold 2001

Acknowledgements

On June 15, 2015, I was crossing the street from the Lee Congregational Church on my way to the Lee Hill Cemetery. As I walked behind Dad's casket, Pastor Gail Kindberg stopped me on the double yellow line in the middle of Route 155. She said, "Mike, I read your first couple of stories. They are really good. You have to get them published. It's important."

Her fervor startled me. I hadn't placed any special significance on what I had been writing. I had approached Dad's request as a functional task. Then I had distributed copies to friends to help me cope with his passing. But this same sentiment has been repeated to me many times.

Some folks have expressed both appreciation and relief that I'm writing my family history. "I'm glad that you're doing this. New Hampshire has no diversity. These people are clueless. Somebody has to say what this place was like."

Whenever you embark on a project such as this, you find yourself beholden to many people. Sometimes the connection is brief but lasting. Other times, folks are in for the long haul. I was lucky. I've had a group of people who have been honest and sustained my efforts when I have flagged. If somehow I missed you, I'll catch you later.

My best attempt at quantifying my supporters are as follows.

To Messrs. Paul Boynton of Begin with Yes and Dave Bastien, who originally told me to jump off the cliff into the world of writing and publishing.

To the late Harvey Woodward and his wife Laurie Legard. Harvey prodded me gently, and Laurie somewhat less so, to continue writing and "tell it like it was."

To two very different people whom I have never met. Ms. Chris Rice is a retired accountant and a cancer survivor. Mr. Bobby West is a cattleman and veteran with Gulf War Syndrome. They are both "fighting the good fight." Their inner strength and conviction has refueled my own.

To the crews at Water St. Bookstore in Exeter and Riverrun Bookstore in Portsmouth, thank you for your support.

To Ms. Angela Petrigni-Ladd, Ms. Sidney Lanier, Messrs. Jon Moss, Michael Provost, and Brian Ward who assisted with the production of the live preview performances of this book.

To Mr. Ted Davis for his assistance with story tuning and focus, especially for my live performances.

To Mr. Richard White, Ph.D., for editing the early drafts.

To my neighbor, Ms. Katrinka Blickle Pellecchia, for final editing and critical analysis.

To my friend, Ms. Prudence Brighton, for her editing and advice throughout this project.

To Mr. Jerrold Cote, for proofreading and editing the final draft.

To the National WWII Museum, for allowing me to use Harold's quote from their 2015 Annual Report in "We're going to Texas.

To the owners and employees of these establishments who have supported this project by allowing me to read story drafts to their patrons:

In Newmarket, NH: American Legion Post #67, Crackskulls, The Big Bean, Panzanella's, Johnny Boston's International, The Oak House, The Riverworks, and last, but certainly not least, The Stone Church.

In Portsmouth, NH: Book and Bar

In Northwood, NH: Umami

To the countless electronic friends on social media and the individuals I've met in the physical world who have read and critiqued my "works in progress." I couldn't have done it without you.

And finally, to all my readers who have purchased, read, appreciated, shared, commented on, and felt a connection to these stories of New Hampshire.

Thank you all.

--Michael Cameron Ward

What's Next

Virginia Elizabeth (White) Ward was my mother.

She was an individual; she did not join the herd.
She was artistic, kind, gentle and dynamic.
She imposed high standards of performance and demanded that they be met.
She understood that you cannot be diminished when you maintain the high ground.
She understood that when you are in the right, nothing can change that calculus.
She understood that when you are in the right, you must be relentless and never back down.
She would not be intimidated.
She shared her knowledge, be it verbal, or requiring physical effort.
When she was faced with a situation that she knew nothing about, she researched it.
She learned from her mistakes.
She was willing to laugh at her shortcomings.
She exemplified grace under pressure.

She was the "Titanium Rose" in Dad's fisted glove. The next volume of Sketches of Lee will be her story, "Titanium Rose".

Biography: Michael Cameron Ward

I graduated in 1976 with a BA in Theatre Arts from the University of New Hampshire. As often with B.A. graduates, I tried several different fields and eventually settled into a 25-year career as a Software Release Engineer at Hewlett-Packard, Cisco Systems, SAP, and the FAA.

Michael Cameron Ward

A Software Release Engineer is required to precisely communicate and record information. In practice, this means creating some of the most boring writing you'll ever read. Nothing in the finished product contains a scrap of humor or emotion, but through that work the desire to write something meaningful was born. At times I indulged in my desire, with an occasional anecdotal story about my life experiences.

I never really expected to become a writer, but that changed on May 20, 2015. My father, Harold Ward, aged 94 was in declining health. With only weeks to live, he made a request: "Michael, I want you to write the stories of our existence. I want my great grandchildren to know from whence they came."

I sat beside Dad's bed on the 4th floor of Exeter Hospital as he recounted life events that he had never told to anyone before. These stories, if not captured, would simply disappear from our family's and country's history. I had written the first two stories before his death on June 9, 2015. He liked them both.

Dad knew that I was a storyteller before he requested that I write our family history. But there is a huge difference between letting it rip extemporaneously and writing it down. Satisfying his request also brought the realization that my accounting had to be truthful, no matter what the pain. Describing other people's actions is simple. It is not so easy to discuss your own actions and emotions. It has been difficult for me to refrain from editorializing to buffer the more difficult events in our history, but I have.

After some close friends read my drafts, they insisted that the stories be published professionally. I resisted them; "What do friends know?" Then in April 2017, I was asked if Mr. Paul Boynton, author of Begin with Yes, could re-post my story *A*

Colored Man in Exeter on his Facebook page with two million followers. The incredible feedback from people I didn't even know inspired me.

It had once seemed incomprehensible that there would be interest in the Ward family history. But that thought was banished by kind words. Hence, the *Sketches of Lee* collection was born.

The first book, *A Colored Man in Exeter*, was published on September 1, 2017. It traced Dad's family history, his childhood, his U.S. Navy career, and his integration of the Exeter, New Hampshire restaurant trade.

Volume II, *The Colored Folks Ain't Gonna Make It*, captures our ignominious retreat from the gangs in Brooklyn to a dirt road in Lee, New Hampshire in 1957. Upon arrival, we became the "index of integration" for the school district and several surrounding towns. Most of the events in this book are sited at our home, Solar Vista."

I'm proud to share these stories with you. I hope that they provide you with a perspective on what it's like to be a pioneer in a foreign land. That's what Harold and Virginia would have wanted.

--Michael Cameron Ward

Michael lives in Lee, New Hampshire at Solar Vista, the family homestead. He shares his environment with the local wildlife population of turkeys, opossums, bears, coyotes, woodchucks, squirrels and others that wander onto the property.

CPSIA information can be obtained
at www.ICGtesting.com
Printed in the USA
JSHW010940021019
1731JS00001B/1